Being Truly Human

Being Truly Human

The Desert Way of Spiritual Formation

Mark Mah

RESOURCE *Publications* • Eugene, Oregon

BEING TRULY HUMAN
The Desert Way of Spiritual Formation

Copyright © 2012 Mark Mah. All rights reserved. Except for brief quotations in critical publications or reviews, no part of this book may be reproduced in any manner without prior written permission from the publisher. Write: Permissions, Wipf and Stock Publishers, 199 W. 8th Ave., Suite 3, Eugene, OR 97401.

Resource Publications
An Imprint of Wipf and Stock Publishers
199 W. 8th Ave., Suite 3
Eugene, OR 97401
www.wipfandstock.com

ISBN 13: 978-1-62032-493-6
Manufactured in the U.S.A.

All Scripture quotations, unless otherwise noted, are from the New International Version of the Bible.

To Joy, and our children:
Sarah, Matthew, and Michael.

Contents

Acknowledgments ix

INTRODUCTION 1

CHAPTER 1   THE HOMELESS SELF 7
    We Have Lost our Way Home
    We Live for Consumption
    Where is our *Axis Mundi?*
    The Homemade Self
    Losing Touch with our True Self
    Confession and Repentance
    The Way to Come Home

CHAPTER 2   ENTERING THE EMPTINESS 23
    Idols of our Heart
    The Call of the Desert
    Make Space for God
    Abandonment of Language
    Abandonment of Self
    Abandonment of Neighbor
    The Deserts of our Life
    Desert Detours

CHAPTER 3   SOLITUDE AND SILENCE 41
    Go and Sit in your Cell
    An Inner World of Chaos
    Giving God our Undivided Attention
    The Use of the Prayer Word
    The Source of our Confidence

Contents

    Prayer of the Mind
    The Power of Silence
    The Night of the Soul
    The Gift of Indifference
    The Gift of Attentiveness

CHAPTER 4   BEING TRULY HUMAN 58
    Freedom to Love
    Giving Attention to Another
    Manifestations of Humility
    Humility is Truthful Living
    Hospitality is to Make Ourselves Available
    Hospitality in Different Worlds
    Hospitality to the Marginalized
    Conclusion

Appendix A   Silent Retreat: Making Space for God in our Busy Lives 83
Appendix B   The Practice of Lectio Divina 85
Bibliography 87

Acknowledgments

THIS BOOK WAS BIRTHED after I taught a course on Desert Spirituality in 2004. The following year, I took the opportunity to write my first draft when I had my sabbatical. At that time, I had no intention to publish. I wrote basically for my own personal edification and reflection on my journey with God. At the same time, I began practicing the discipline of solitude and silence. Since then I had organized silent retreats for my students who found the retreats refreshing and helpful to their spiritual life. Their positive input was an encouragement and a challenge for me to continue with this journey. I seriously decided to rewrite and make major revisions to my original draft at the end of 2011. I am grateful to my students who have inspired and surprised me on many occasions. My thanks go to the Malaysia Baptist Theological Seminary for giving me the opportunity and freedom to teach the course on Spiritual Formation. I also want to thank Lian Kee for her kind consent to proofread the manuscript. Last, but not least, I want to thank my wife, Joy, for being a friend and faithful companion all these years.

Introduction

> Midway along the journey of our life I woke to find myself in a dark wood, for I had wandered off from the straight path.
>
> —Dante Alighieri[1]

There is a story of a man who having lost a key to his house began searching for it in his garden. His neighbors saw his problem and helped him with the search. They went down on their hands and knees searching for the lost key. They could not find the missing key. Finally they asked him where he thought he might have lost the key. "I lost the key inside the house," he replied. "Then why are you searching for it outside in the garden?" the neighbors asked out of curiosity. Without a moment's hesitation, he replied, "Because there is light out here!"

The story is hilarious, but it brings home a fundamental truth: we tend to seek truth in the wrong places. The key is inside the house and not outside in the garden. The key that unlocks the door to our spirituality is within the depths of our soul and not outside of us. I was taught to believe that doing is all it takes to develop my spirituality. Involvement is the key to grow my spiritual life. We gauge our spirituality based on how busy and active we are in the Lord's work. I wince when Christians remark to me how busy they are. Our busy exterior may be a cover-up for an undernourished interior soul. Jesus reminds us that God's kingdom is within us, and the kingdom of God will not come

---

1. Alighieri, *The Divine Comedy: Inferno*, 67.

to us unless we spend time cultivating our inner life by making room for him in our hearts. The advice of Thomas a Kempis, who wrote *The Imitation of Christ* in the fifteenth century, is still valid for us today. He gives this advice: "Learn indifference to all that lies outside of you and devote yourself to the life within, and you will see the kingdom of God coming to you."[2]

We need to be awakened to the desire that God has planted in our hearts in order to begin the inward journey in the wilderness of our soul. David Benner, a psychologist and spiritual coach, points out that this desire is at the center of our spiritual life and indispensable for our journey to being truly human. Guilt may motivate us to behave christianly, or obligation may lead us to spend time and money in God's work, but only desire can get us to begin the inward journey and lead us along the way.[3] This desire, if not properly identified and appropriated, can cause us to become restless and lead us astray. Like the man in the story, our restlessness can lead us to find the key in the wrong places. It can lead us on the wrong path. Dante Alighieri, a fourteenth century Italian poet and philosopher, in the opening words of his *Divine Comedy*, describes the common predicament of getting lost and trapped by life. The poem depicts a journey Dante has to make to reach his true home in paradise. In the middle of his life, Dante awakes to the reality that he has lost his way in a dark wood. He discovers that he has wandered off the straight path without knowing about it. Like Dante, most of us sleep through life and have lost the way.

I was awakened from my slumber by the lingering dissatisfaction I had with my brand of Christianity that thrived on doing and very little on being. Activity was a gauge of spirituality. The degree of my commitment in God's work was a measure of my spirituality. I had reached a point in my spiritual life that I needed to do something in order to grow. This desire, aroused by a lingering disappointment with formal Christianity, led me

2. Kempis, *The Imitation of Christ*, 83.
3. Benner, *Soulful Spirituality*, 15.

to seek inspiration outside and beyond my tradition. I realize that mine is not an isolated case. William Hendricks did a research based on interviews with believers who stopped attending church. In his book, *Exit Interviews,* he concludes that spiritually starved Christians failed to find God in the maze of church programs. Disillusioned and discouraged, they left to search for God outside its walls.[4] I was attracted to the Desert Fathers because they too were reacting to a Christianity weakened by worldly and powerful interests. In order to free themselves from the shackles of a corrupted, decadent society and a worldly Church, they entered the desert to recover the ideals of Christianity.

Pilgrims do not travel alone. They need each other's company to make the journey meaningful and less monotonous. The exchange and interaction between travelers will clear the vision, ease the conscience, and strengthen the resolve to continue on the journey. Past and present saints have travelled the path that I am treading now. They are my fellow pilgrims. We share a common passion for God though we come from different backgrounds, traditions, and theological persuasions. Each traveler has a story to tell, an experience to share, and an adventure to talk about. They encourage, refresh, and inspire each other when the journey gets tough and threatening. I am acquainted with these saints through the books they write. Many of them lived in the past, but there are contemporaries as well.

It was Henri Nouwen's book, *The Way of the Heart,* which first introduced me to the Desert Fathers. While commenting on how tough it is for ministers to serve numbed congregations at the end of the twentieth century, he looks to a more primitive source of inspiration: the Desert Fathers who lived in the Egyptian desert during the fourth and fifth centuries. He feels that the Desert Fathers' directness, simplicity, and concreteness to life's struggles provide a fresh perspective for his contemporaries. Belden Lane's book, *The Solace of Fierce Landscapes,* opened my eyes to the virtues and practice of desert spirituality. He explains

4. Hendricks, *Exit Interviews,* chaps. 1, 19.

why seekers of God are drawn to the silence and solitude of harsh terrains. Fierce landscapes, like the desert, can abandon and also offer solace and healing to the broken soul. The indifference of wilderness will help me shed my false self and free me from the neurotic need for attention in order to become more human.

From Craig Barnes' book, *Searching for Home*, I learned that the nomadic soul was homesick and always yearning for home. He writes, "The most enduring trace of God in our lives is our longing for home that wells up in our soul."[5] Unless the soul awakes to the fact that God is calling him to his true home within the depths of his soul, his homesickness will lead him down to many different paths. Jean Vanier's book, *Becoming Human*, challenges me to be more open to outsiders like the marginalized in society. I will enjoy personal freedom and become more human when I overcome my fears and learn to trust others through inclusion. This inclusion respects and values the worth of each person who is made in God's image. I need to learn to treat each person as an important, unique, and sacred individual.

The ideas and experiences of these fellow pilgrims inspire and challenge me, and the writing of this book reflects that. I am grateful for such companions who walk with me along this path as we head for our true home. Home is where we are in touch with our true selves that cause us to become more human. This book is for seekers of God who find the contemporary religious scene too suffocating, shallow, and superficial for the good of their souls. They want something more and are willing to make the sacrifices and take the risks needed to journey with God in the wilderness of their soul. This book has four chapters.

The first chapter explains why we have lost our way home. Along the way, we manufacture our own homemade identity that thrives on consumption rather than communion. We assume many different identities and roles while living in a consumer culture that has replaced religion as its center. These add stress and dissatisfaction to our well-being. We have lost touch with

---

5. Barnes, *Searching for Home*, 21.

Introduction

our true identities. We need to be awakened to our dire situation, confess our lost condition, and return home like the prodigal son. This will not be easy. The way home requires us to yield and surrender our identity that leads to the demise of our false, homemade self.

The second chapter urges us to take heed to the call of the desert, but we have to deal with the idols in our heart first. Idolatry is when we confine or reduce God to a manageable level for our own needs. Desert spirituality does not promote a religion of self-actualization but the denial of self. The call of the desert is a call to emptiness. It is to empty ourselves in order to make space for God in our hearts. It is a call to the abandonment of self, language, and neighbor. We do not need to enter a real desert to get rid of the false self. The discipline of solitude and silence will help us to create a "wilderness" in our soul.

The third chapter dwells on the need to practice solitude and silence in our life. This will not be easy because when we leave the world behind us, an inner world of chaos opens up on us. Some general guidelines and observations are highlighted to help those we want to grow in the discipline. We are so used to verbal and mental prayer that silent prayer in solitude can be quite a challenge for many people. The effects of this discipline are felt outside the time of solitude and silence in our daily lives. The consistent practice of this discipline will produce the twin gifts of indifference and attentiveness that will free us to love and become truly human.

The last chapter focuses on what it means to be truly and deeply human. To be truly human is to love freely. If we do not have freedom, love becomes manipulative and is conditioned by our need for control and affection. Genuine love is giving attention to others without any hidden agenda or giving judgment. The desert virtues of humility and hospitality are expressions of genuine love. Humility opens a space for the other party to speak and calls us to enter into obedience to the other person. Hospitality is to make ourselves available and be fully present to the other person. This chapter also highlights the need to create a hospitable space in the home, the school, the workplace, and with the marginalized. To be fully human is to free ourselves from the compulsive self. This will lead us to play a constructive and effective role in making the world a better place with little expectations of results and rewards in return.

Following the words of the prophet Jeremiah, this book is calling on God's children to consider the ancient paths taken by the Desert Fathers:

> Stand at the crossroads and look; ask for the ancient paths, ask where the good way is, and walk in it, and you will find rest for your souls.[6]

If you are a seeker of God and is passionate about the spiritual development of your life, this book may lead you on a journey to full personhood. It may be the answer to your restless search for fulfillment and happiness in life. In taking to the ancient paths of earlier saints, you may find rest for your restless souls when you walk with them along the good way.

---

6. Jer 6:16.

Chapter 1

The Homeless Self

> You have made us to be toward Yourself, O Lord, and our hearts are restless until they rest in You.
>
> —AUGUSTINE OF HIPPO[1]

We have Lost our Way Home

SINCE THE TIME OUR first parents fell into sin, our memory of home is vague though our longing for paradise remains strong. God's first question to Adam when banished from the garden was, "Where are you?" Man lost his intimacy with God through sin but not all was lost. There remains a longing within man's heart to return home. The book of Ecclesiastes rightly observes that God has set eternity in the hearts of men; they will remain restless and dissatisfied until they make their way home. Home is not about getting to the right place; it is about having a right relationship. For those who love and obey him, Jesus promises that he and the Father will come to them and make their home with them.[2]

The first sin in the Bible is about Cain and his brother Abel. Cain got jealous because God favored Abel. Blinded by

---

1. Augustine, *The Confessions of Saint Augustine*, 15.
2. John 14:23.

uncontrollable rage, Cain killed his brother. That was the first murder recorded in history. As a result God put a curse on Cain. The earth would no longer yield crops, and he would be a restless wanderer. The curse is two-fold.[3] His work would be unfulfilling no matter how much Cain put in his work. Dissatisfied with life, he would continue seeking and searching with the vain hope that he would finally get what he looked for all his life.

Man's restless search leads him to live a mazelike existence. Every hedge, corner, and turn in a maze looks identical. Frustrations set in after numerous attempts to leave the maze end in failure. Each retreat and turn give hope, but a dead end quickly dashes hope. He tries again hoping that the next turn will lead him out of the maze. By making many false starts and desperate turns, he dashes from place to place with the hope that the next one will finally work for him. Symptoms of a mazelike life are everywhere: getting a new job because the old one did not meet his expectations, a second marriage because the first one did not work, a new place because the old had too many unpleasant memories, a new appearance because the old looked stale and unexciting, or a new skill because the old became irrelevant. Life in a maze is like on a treadmill—moving somewhere but getting nowhere. Blaise Pascal, a French mathematician and Christian philosopher, is right when he says that man is not living but hoping to live.

Man does not think that he is lost in a maze. Though frustrated at times, he treasures the freedom to choose at each fork of the road. Such freedom carries a price tag. The idea of making choices often leads to anxiety, fear, and isolation. The thought of making the wrong choice and paying dearly for the consequences frightens him. Yet he is willing to be enslaved by freedom in exchange for a life filled with dreams and hope. In Dostoyevsky's book, *The Brothers Karamazov*, the Grand Inquisitor said to Jesus Christ:

---

3. Barnes, *Searching for Home*, 34.

> There has never been anything more difficult for man and human society to bear than freedom . . . In the end they will lay their freedom at our feet and say to us, "Enslave us, but feed us!"[4]

We have not changed much since Dostoyevsky's time. Our appetite has gone beyond food to consumer products and services that will make our dreams come true. We are hoping to live a life based on consumption thinking that this will satisfy our inner longings for home.

We Live for Consumption

Joseph Stowell relates this story about his three and a half years old Matthew who got lost while Christmas shopping in a suburban mall. His wife, dad, and mum went different directions to search for Matthew. Having given up hope of finding Matthew at the assigned place, he went back to look for others.

> Unsuccessful, I trudged back to our meeting point. My wife, Martie, had not found him, nor had my mother. And then my dad appeared, holding little Matthew by the hand. Our hearts leapt for joy. Interestingly enough, Matthew was untraumatized. He hadn't been crying. To him, there had been no problem. I asked my father where he had found him. "The candy counter," he replied. "You should have seen him. His eyes came just about as high as the candy. He held his little hands behind his back and moved his head back and forth, surveying all the luscious options." Matthew didn't look lost. He didn't know he was lost. He was oblivious to the phenomenal danger he was in. This is a candy-counter culture, where people who don't look lost and don't know they're lost live for consumption.[5]

---

4. Cited by Barnes, *Searching for Home,* 94. See Dostoyevsky, *The Brothers Karamazov,* 304–5.
5. Stowell, "Candy Counter Culture," *Moody Monthly,* 4.

We live for consumption. Consumerism has become a substitute religion. It promises to fulfill our most fundamental needs which are religious—our need for God. In the old days, the church or cathedral was the most prominent building in the town or village. It was the center of activities and all traffic led to it. The modern cathedrals are the shopping malls of today. Most likely, a primitive Christian when faced with trouble would go to a church to pray. Unfortunately, a modern Christian when depressed will go to a shopping mall to forget her woes. Like attending church, people dutifully and faithfully track to the mall at least once a week for supplies. The design of the mall is to tempt and entice us with the promise to satisfy our deepest needs and longings. The gospel of commercialism keeps blaring and flashing into our ears and eyes. It says, "Use me, take me, buy me, drink me, smell me, touch me, kiss me, sleep with me."[6] Slick images with catchy captions loudly promise to match our every need. Whether it is insecurity, worry, pain, curiosity, pride, or appetite, there is a product out there to soothe us, boost our esteem, gratify our ego, and keep us satisfied and happy. Unfortunately the promise to fulfill our deepest needs is short-lived. The first big ticket item for people who live in a car culture is to own a car. We are happy and gratified when we get our hands on the steering wheel of our first car, but the second car we own must be better and bigger than the first. If not we will feel dissatisfied and disappointed. Our needs, like the grave, are never satisfied.

Consumption, as a substitute religion, can be addictive and leads to a compulsive lifestyle. Consumerism is about making choices, and we relish the freedom to choose. But there is a dark side to it as pointed out by Anthony Giddens, a social scientist. In his book, *Runaway World*, he writes, "The dark side of decision making is the rise of addictions and compulsions."[7] It is not strange that in a consumer-driven society people going for counseling and therapy are on the rise. We look to consumer

---

6. Nouwen, *The Way of the Heart*, 45–46.
7. Giddens, *Runaway World*, 46.

products for self-gratification. In the process we are in bondage to them. Addiction takes place even before we come to recognize it. We know that we are addicted when we look at these products or services expecting gratification and to want more of them. We are addicted when the absence of these products or services is greatly missed affecting right away our mood and feelings. The narcotic of consumption will lead us to the next fix, but this will not last for long. A narcotic has no choice but is always looking out for better pay, better job, higher standard of living, and a more promising future, in order to maintain his addiction.

Where is our *Axis Mundi*?

Life revolves around a single, sacred pole (or totem) in a primitive society. This pole, that extends to the center of the earth and to the heavens above, functions as the axle around which the world revolves. Religion, that binds the heavens and earth together, provides the stabilizing force that life in general needs. Primitive people are religious for the simple reason that life, without the aid of modern science and technology, is too unpredictable and fragile without its *axis mundi*.[8] The Temple of Heaven in Beijing, China provides such a symbol at the time of the emperors. The iconic building is on a foundation that has a semi-circle and a half square joined together. The semi-circle represents the heavens above and the square the earth below. The Temple of Heaven symbolizes the pivotal point that holds the heavens and the earth together. It is the "totem pole" for the nation of China. Twice a year the emperor would stay a night there, preparing himself through a ritual of ceremonial cleansing and fasting, to offer sacrifices to heaven with the hope and prayers that the coming harvest would be a good one.

The identity of primitive people is tied to the place they stay and to the community they live. If we ask a primitive person

---

8. Latin word which means "the axle which the world revolves."

who he is, he will answer that he is a son of so-and-so and lives in a particular village. He can also tell you about the people in the village and how they are related to him. The place and the people who live there have an existence tied permanently to the *axis mundi*. Once we went on a mission trip to a remote village in Sarawak, Malaysia. We were heading towards Long Napir which was the home village of one of the members of the mission team. When our four-wheel drive was approaching Long Napir on a dusty and bumpy road, we began asking questions. We were curious about our surroundings, being city people, and queried the brother about the place that passed us. Each time he would reply that such and such a place belonged to one of the villagers. The surprising thing was that there were no markers indicating ownership. He instinctively knew the people and place even though he no longer stayed there. We had a good laugh. In a modern city, we do not even know who our neighbors are.

Modern society has lost its *axis mundi*. We have taken on a new identity when we are lost and adrift from home. When we do not belong to a place or people, we drift along and are rootless. Change is the norm rather than the exception when not rooted to a permanent center. We change clothes according to the season or fashion. Gadgets are not to last because we change them for new and better ones under the lure of clever advertising and improved technology. Relationships will not last either. The divorce rate has risen and more and more children come from single parent homes. Easy access to cheap and efficient transport increases people's mobility nowadays. It is difficult for us to forge lasting friendships knowing that we will not be in the same place for long. Life in a mobile society tends to be shallow and artificial. No wonder Simone Weil, a French philosopher and mystic, observes that rootedness is the most important and least recognized need of the human soul.[9] Thomas Kelly, a Quaker and author of the spiritual classic, *A Testament of Devotion*, has this to say:

9. Weil, *The Need for Roots*, 3.

> We are not skilled in the inner life where the real roots of our problem lie . . . The outer distractions of our interests reflect an inner lack of integration of our own selves. We are trying to be several selves at once, without all our selves being organized by a single, mastering Life within us.[10]

Not able to recognize that to be rooted is one of the greatest needs of the human soul, the modern person moves from place to place, job to job, relationship to relationship, picking up different identities along the way. He lives in many worlds and plays different roles at any one time. If we ask a modern person who he is, he answers in many different ways depending on who he is talking to. He will say that he is a doctor or mechanic, plays golf or tennis, a married man, a divorcee or single parent, a member of the PTA in his daughter's school, enjoys a game of bridge or chess, and occasionally plays the saxophone with a local band. The plurality of roles and identities make modern living stressful and empty of meaning and purpose. The consumer is being consumed. Our identity is derived from God because we bear his image. With "nothing of eternity at its core,"[11] we look to other sources for our identity. According to Athanasius, a fourth century bishop, this results in an empty feeling in our soul.[12] We want more and look for more things to possess or do to fill this emptiness with the hope that much doing, wanting, and having will numb the pain and fill the void in our heart.

The Homemade Self

True happiness is elusive to the empty soul. This does not stop people from pursuing after happiness. The modern person's identity is self-constructed. It is a homemade self that he has nurtured from young. At a young age, he has instinctively developed this idea that he can only be happy if his fundamental needs are

10. Kelly, *A Testament of Devotion*, 91.
11. Barnes, *Searching for Home*, 57.
12. Athanasius, "On the Incarnation," 57.

met. What are these needs? They are the needs for security and survival, esteem and affection, and power and control.[13]

A child's basic needs are for survival and security. When a child is hungry, he cries and wants milk to ease his hunger. The mother, sensing this need, readily supplies milk from her breasts. She carries the baby close to her chest. The child, while sucking milk, stops crying when he feels the warm and softness of the mother's breast. This not only eases his hunger pains but also gives him a feeling of security. For this reason, breast milk is far better than powdered milk for young babies. Besides having better nutrients, breast milk also gives better emotional support for the child.

His basic needs change when the child becomes a teenager. His need for survival and security has taken a backstage to the need for esteem and affection. At this stage of his life, he begins to show interest in his outward appearance (especially in front of the opposite sex) and is conscious of what he wears and how he styles his hair. He spends long moments in front of the mirror brushing up his appearance in order to look his best in front of his peers. His esteem is dependent on how his peers view him. He easily yields to peer-pressure wanting to be accepted and be popular. For this reason, he takes the peer's counsel more seriously than his own parents. He begins to exert his independence from parental control and turns rebellious. He falls in love for the first time because he wants to be noticed and yearns for affection.

An adult's instinctive need is for power and control. Most adults, at this time, will work hard at their job in order to get a promotion. A higher position in the factory or company means a bigger income and more power and control over the subordinates. A bigger salary means more spending power, financial stability, and a better grip on one's unpredictable life. It is not strange that career goals, at this stage of his life, become a priority that take over much of his time, effort, and resources. Frustrations set

---

13. I am indebted to Thomas Keating for this section on the "homemade self." See Keating, *The Human Condition*, 13–14.

in when he feels that his career is stagnating and prospects are dim. He may even be thinking of switching job or even a change in vocational direction at some point in his adult life. This is in order to get a fresh start with the hope that things may work out differently in his favor.

According to Thomas Keating, a Trappist monk, this self-constructed, homemade identity revolves around a private universe.[14] We like to sing this worship song, "It's all about you, Lord," when referring to Jesus. This new identity sings a different tune, "It's all about me." The marketplace uses this slogan to bring home the point, "The customer is always right!" Making the customer happy is the number one priority. "What is there for me?" is the catchword. Any stimulus that comes from the outside is rejected or welcomed based on whether it can make the self happy or sad. The self is king. All things, including its needs and wants, revolve around it. Ironically this homemade, false self is programmed not for happiness but for misery. Our false sense of happiness is based on what we have and do or what people act, say, or think about us. We become angry when people accuse us of wrong doing and say unkind words to us. We are ready to receive praise but not rejection. Our self esteem is hurt, and we think that we are not loved. We feel frustrated and depressed when our anticipated promotion does not materialize, and our dream of the new car vaporizes into thin air. When we lose our job, we fear for our survival and future security. We feel threatened because we are losing power and control. Listening to our own voice or the voices of others instead of God's voice will lead us to a false sense of self.

In the wilderness, Jesus faced the temptation to listen to his own voice and that of Satan's. He was tempted three times. The first was to turn stone into bread because he was hungry. If Jesus listened to his hunger pangs, he would have yielded to Satan's suggestion to turn stone into bread. He then quoted Scripture by saying, "Man does not live on bread alone." The first temptation

---

14. Keating, *The Human Condition*, 13–14.

tested his sense of survival and security. The second test was to jump from a high tower in the temple. This time Satan got the cue and used Scripture to entice Jesus. He said, "If you are the Son of God, throw yourself down from here, for it is written, 'He will command his angels concerning you to guard you carefully; they will lift you up in their hands, so that you will not strike your foot against a stone.'" This daredevil act appealed to Jesus' sense of esteem and affection. When news about his great feat made the headlines, he would be a popular hero who will be highly esteemed by the people. Again Jesus preferred to listen to God's voice by appealing to Scripture, saying, "Do not put the Lord your God to the test." The third test aimed at Jesus' sense of power and control. Satan promised to give Jesus all the kingdoms of the world, along with their authority and splendor, if he would just worship him. The third test was the most appealing. Jesus could have the crown without the cross. One more time, Jesus appealed to Scripture by listening to God's voice. He said, "Worship the Lord your God and serve him only." If Jesus had yielded to these temptations, he would have given way to his false self. He did not because he only listened to his Father.

Henri Nouwen, a noted spiritual writer, points out that this false self is dictated by anger and greed:

> When my sense of self depends on what others say of me, anger is a quite natural reaction to a critical word. And when my sense of self depends on what I can acquire, greed flares up when my desires are frustrated. Thus, greed and anger are the brother and sister of a false self fabricated by the social compulsions of an unredeemed world.[15]

---

15. Nouwen, *Way of the Heart*, 23.

Losing Touch with our True Self

The parable of the Prodigal Son tells the story of a father with two sons: one is greedy of his father's wealth and the other is angry at his father's benevolence.[16] Both carry within themselves a false self fabricated by the compulsions of the world. The younger son is greedy of his father's wealth and wants a share of his inheritance prematurely. Unwilling to wait any longer, he boldly requests for his share of inheritance. Surprisingly his father agrees to let him have his part. Away from home, he spends his wealth in wild living and squanders his money away. He loses all he has and is in great need. At the end he finds himself feeding the pigs at a farm. The elder brother in the story is angry that his father slaughters a fattened calf to celebrate the younger son's homecoming. He should be the one deserving it rather than his prodigal brother who has squandered the father's wealth. It is unfair for him to endure all the hard work, while his younger brother is enjoying life patronizing prostitutes!

What is wrong with both of them? Both have lost touch with their true identities as sons of the father. The younger son rejects the love of the father by leaving home and taking on a new identity in a distant country. He refuses to acknowledge his need for his father and wants to live independently of him. Far away from home, he yields to his worldly desires and takes up a different lifestyle. His newfound happiness does not last long. It lasts as long as he can pay the mounting bills. Having rejected the father's love, he keeps searching for a substitute to replace the void in his heart. He search leads him to all kinds of wild indulgences that can only bring temporary satisfaction.

The older brother, though at home with the father, refuses to accept his love. The father's love is always extended to him. "All I have is yours," the father tells him. He rather works hard to earn his father's acceptance. Thinking that he is not worthy of his father's love, he needs to prove his own worth before him. He tries

---

16. See Luke 15: 11–32.

hard to win the favor and attention of his father by his dutiful labors. He gets angry when he sees his younger brother getting all the attention of the father when he comes home. Perceiving that he is not treated fairly, he strongly protests, "Look! All these years I've been slaving for you and never disobeyed your orders. Yet you never gave me even a young goat, so I could celebrate with my friends."

The turning point of the story is when the prodigal awakens to the reality of his lost condition. This comes about when he thinks of the home he leaves behind. He comes to his senses when he remembers that the servants at his father's house have more than enough to eat. Here he is hungry and fighting with the pigs for scraps of spoiled, rotten food. When a person knows that he is lost, the next thing is for him to find his way home. This is what the prodigal decides to do. Having refused the father's love, he is not so sure that he will receive back this love: the love he rejected in the first place. He will not mind if his father decides to treat him as one of his servants. With confession on his lips that he is lost and repentance in his heart that he deserves his father's judgment, he gets up and returns home. The father is ready to welcome his long lost son into his arms. He has been looking forward to this day for a long while. He finds back his lost son and quickly asks for the best robe to put on him. He then puts a ring on his finger and sandals on his feet. The prodigal has lost touch of his true identity, and the father is doing all these things to remind his son of his true status. He is not a servant of the house, but a true son beloved of the father. That calls for a celebration. On the other hand, the older brother has yet to discover and be in touch with his true identity. Unlike his prodigal brother, he is still lost and not yet found.

Confession and Repentance

As beloved children of God, we see ourselves on a spiritual journey with the quest to "become who we are."[17] We can only begin this journey when we reckon with these two questions: "Where am I?" and "Who am I?" God put forth the first question to our first parents when they lost their intimacy with him in the garden. Like the prodigal, we must acknowledge that we are lost in a distant country and far away from home. Unless we awake to this reality, we cannot begin the journey home. One of George Orwell's essays offers a graphic picture of human lostness. In it, Orwell describes a wasp:

> It was sucking jam on my plate and I cut him in half. He paid no attention, merely went on with his meal, while a tiny stream of jam trickled out of his severed esophagus. Only when he tried to fly away did he grasp the dreadful thing that happened to him.[18]

Lost people are like the wasp. Unaware and severed from their souls, they continue to consume life's sweetness out of greed. The wasp finally grasped its dreadful condition when it tried to fly. Likewise we are aware of our lost condition through crisis moments in our life. Like the prodigal son, a crisis forces us to the awareness of our lost condition and calls us to leave our restless wanderings to come home. The next question, we need to reckon with, concerns our self-identity. Who am I? We make the mistake of allowing our identity to be formed by others. We have a neurotic need for approval from significant others in our life. Our false self likes to play to the gallery. We perform for them assuming that we are the center of their attention. We are concerned about what they think of us and how they perceive us. All this while, we do not realize that we are playing to an imaginary

---

17. Nouwen, *Life of the Beloved*, 26.
18. Cited by L'Engle in her novel, *A Severed Wasp*. The title of her book is taken from a quote found in a book review by George Orwell.

and invisible audience that is not there at all. As Anthony de Mello confesses:

> Before I was twenty, I never worried about what other people thought of me. But after I was twenty I was worried endlessly—about all the impressions I made and how people were evaluating me. Only sometime after turning fifty, did I realize that they hardly ever thought about me at all.[19]

The elder brother in the story of the Prodigal Son works slavishly to earn the approval of his father. He wants to show his father that he is a responsible and filial person who is worthy to be called his son. We too look to God for approval. God is like a father who is both demanding and hard to please. We refuse his embrace of love but work hard to earn his love. In the process, we have formed a false image of ourselves.

    We need confession and repentance before we can begin the journey home. We need to confess that we are indeed lost and are awakened to the reality that we need to find the way home. Repentance requires us to make an about turn. This is not easy even for those who are awakened to their lost condition. We live and believe in the lie for so long that we prefer living in hell than in heaven. C. S. Lewis, in *The Great Divorce*, paints a story of ghosts who are given the opportunity to leave hell and climb a mountain to paradise. At first the journey is difficult because the terrain is not friendly to ghosts' feet. As they make progress, the journey becomes easier when their feet become firm and real. Many ghosts do not make it because they keep looking back to hell. There is a ghost who has a terrible lizard on his shoulder. The lizard has stayed there for so long that the ghost has befriended his tormentor. The lizard hates the journey and keeps nagging the ghost to return "home" in hell. An angel is waiting to kill it but only with the consent of the ghost. The ghost hesitates. He has been with the lizard for so long that the thought of leaving it

---

19. Mello, *One Minute Wisdom*, 91.

frightens him. He either continues with the journey or returns. He finally decides to get rid of the lizard. In a twinkling of an eye, the angel slays the lizard. The ghost immediately becomes a man, and the lizard transforms into a white stallion that carries the man all the way up the mountain.[20]

The Way to Come Home

We need to make an about turn in order to shed the false self and take on the true self. According to the apostle Paul, we need to put off the "old man," in order to put on the "new man." It will not be an easy process. In order to do this, we need to make a journey—a journey with God in the wilderness of the soul. The desert, according to Thomas Merton, has the capacity to "reject completely the false, formal self, fabricated under social compulsion in the world."[21] The old self needs to die to make way for the resurrection of the new self. Whoever finds life will lose it; whoever loses his life will find it.

In his book, *The Solace of Fierce Landscapes*, Belden Lane, a Presbyterian minister, writes about a nineteenth-century dervish teacher, Awad Afifi, who once shared this story with his pupils.[22]

The story of the stream begins when rain began falling on a high mountain in a distant land. Swirling around rocks and trees, it gathered strength as it poured down the slopes. Soon rivulets of water gathered to become a stream. The stream, having left the heights, finally made its way to the edge of the desert. Having crossed barriers before, the stream was expected to overcome this as well. Water kept splashing into the desert, but it vanished quickly into the sand. A voice came from the desert saying, "The stream can cross the desert like the wind." Ignoring the voice, the

---

20. Cited by Barnes, *Searching for Home*, 111–2. See Lewis, *The Great Divorce*, 72–73.

21. Merton, "Wilderness and Paradise," 84.

22. Cited by Lane, *The Solace of Fierce Landscapes*, 21. Adapted from *Tales of the Dervishes*, 23–24.

stream kept splashing into the sand. "You can never cross the desert in this way. You need to let the wind carry you," said the voice. The stream fearing it would lose its identity resisted the advice. If it gave itself to the wind, would it become a stream again? The desert reminded the stream that if it continued flowing into the sand it would become a swamp at the desert's edge. The stream was disturbed by the prospect of being stranded at the desert's edge. While remaining silent, it recalled how waters overcome by yielding: flowing around obstacles and turning to steam when threatened by fire. Slowly, it yielded to the wind by turning itself into vapors to form a cloud. When carried by the wind, the cloud crossed the desert with ease. Soon it was approaching the distant mountains and the stream began falling as light rain. The rainwater on the slopes became rivulets of water, pouring and dashing around rocks and trees, to become a new stream.

In this lovely story, the stream has to give up its identity in order to cross the desert. Refusing to do so means it will never be able to cross over to the other side. By giving up its identity, will it lose it? That is its fear. If it yields to the welcoming arms of the wind, will it be a stream again? The false self must die before the true self can be revealed. We can either get stuck at the desert's edge or closer to home at the other side. The choice is ours to make.

Questions to Consider and Reflect

1. How do you explain this residual restlessness nagging inside you when everything seems to be going well with you?

2. Are there some unresolved problems that cause you pain right now? Do you think God is using some of these to awaken your desire for him?

3. Imagine yourself to be the stream in the story. How will you feel if you are asked to give up your identity in order to continue the journey? What kind of fears and anxieties do you have when you face the unknown journey ahead of you?

Chapter 2

Entering the Emptiness

> I tell you the truth, unless a kernel of wheat
>   falls to the ground and dies, it remains
>   only a single seed. But if it dies, it produces many seeds.
> The man who loves his life
>   will lose it, while the man who hates his life in this world
>   will keep it for eternal life.
>
> —Jesus Christ[1]

Idols of our Heart

WE NEED TO SET aside the idols when we enter the desert. It is difficult to leave them behind when we embark on a journey to the unknown because they give us a sense of safety and nostalgia. This could be the reason why Rachel took Laban's gods when she left with Jacob for his homeland. That was Rachel's first time leaving her country and going to a completely foreign place. The thought of it made her anxious. Jacob might have told Rachel about Esau and his uneasiness about meeting him. Would Esau forgive his brother who had cheated him of his birthright years

---

1. John 12:24–25.

ago? Would his other relatives be like Esau? Rachel, anxious and worried, sought comfort in the gods of her homeland.²

The tendency to idolatry is still strong even in the desert. While Moses met God up on the mountain, Israel made a golden calf at the foot of it. In a harsh environment, lean and mean in resources, the longing for comfort and safety of home grows in us. "There we sat around pots of meat and ate all the food we wanted, but you have brought us out into this desert to starve this entire assembly," complained Israel.³ Idols, like the pets at home, are domesticated gods. We mould and shape them according to our image in order to make them serve us. No wonder we feel comfortable with them around us. We need to face the reality that the desert God cannot be domesticated. At the foot of Mount Sinai, the whole camp trembled at the sight of the mountain. It was filled with billowing smoke, loud thunder, and flashes of lightning when the Lord descended on the cloud covered mountain. The whole mountain trembled violently. The people were told not to go near and touch the side of the mountain for fear that they be struck dead. Like the wild mountain, the God that was on it could not be tamed.

We entertain idols in the heart when we confine or reduce God to a concept, an experience, ongoing projects, or a set of rules.⁴ We reduce God to a concept to cater to the need for clarity and precision because we cannot tolerate any ambiguity in our beliefs. This satisfies us intellectually, but this will not last because we cannot relate to an idea. Logic and abstraction will not satisfy the longings of the heart, for the heart yearns for intimacy and fellowship. In order to satisfy us emotionally, we reduce God to an experience when we get God to cater to the need for sensual pleasure. This God will supply us with waves of intense self-absorbed pleasure. Each encounter calls for an increased degree

---

2. Gen 31:34

3. Exod 16:3.

4. I am indebted to Kerry Walters for his description of "household gods." See Walters, *Soul Wilderness,* 23–44.

of sensation in order to experience the same level of intensity. We become addictive and are looking out for the next fix. God is on call, ready and willing, to meet the endless demands for more. Some of us prefer clear guidelines that dictate the way we conduct ourselves. So we reduce God to a set of rules that tells us in no uncertain terms what we can do and what we cannot do—a list of do's and don'ts. This gives structure and control over our lives, but the hand of God is tied making him too predictable. For those of us who cannot stay still, we use God's name indiscriminately to give legitimacy to our busyness. We find pleasure in our many accomplishments, and we use God for that end. Eugene Peterson, author and professor of spiritual theology, writes:

> Because the ideas and projects have the name of God attached to them, it is easy to assume that we are involved with God. It is the devil's work to get us worked up thinking and acting for God and then subtly detaches us from a relational obedience and adoration of God, substituting ourselves, our godlike egos, in the place originally occupied by God.[5]

The Call of the Desert

Institutionalized Christianity tends to make golden calves out of the true God with the aim to cater to the self-serving needs of its adherents. We do well to take heed to the Apostle John's warning to believers at the end of his letter in the first epistle of John, "Little children, keep yourselves from idols."[6] For me, this call of the desert was aroused by a lingering dissatisfaction with a religion that is too sentimental, sanitized, sterile, and self-serving. The feel-good spirituality of modern-day Christians does not take seriously the call of God to deny self, take up the cross, and follow Jesus. Marketplace Christianity promotes a re-

---

5. Peterson, *Christ Plays in Ten Thousand Places*, 31.
6. See 1 John 5:21.

ligion of self-actualization by using a mix of pop psychology and theology. People love God for the goods and services that God can provide for them. I fully agree with Belden Lane's comment: "I don't really need a God who is solicitous of my every need, fawning for my attention, eager for nothing in the world so much as the fulfillment of my self-potential."[7]

I need a God who can transform me from the inside out. I look for a God who can journey with me in the wilderness of my soul, tearing down every idol in my heart, and making a home there with me. The desert has been the preferred place to train God's servants. The ruggedness of the place calls for a rugged faith in its inhabitants. It is a place of transformation because the souls that dwell there will never be the same again. The Bible has plenty of examples of men and women with rugged faith. Abraham, a man of the city, received a call to leave for the desert country of Canaan. He became the father of many nations. He is the spiritual father of the Jews, Muslims, and Christians. Moses spent forty years in the desert of Midian, in the vicinity of Mount Sinai. Years of desert living changed him from a self-confident prince to a humble shepherd. When he was ready, God chose him to lead Israel out of Egypt to the Promised Land. Before David was ready to become Israel's greatest and most revered king, he had to spend time in the wilderness fleeing from Saul. He learnt humility and patience in the harsh desert environment. In order to rule Israel, he must wait for God's timing.

In the New Testament, John appeared on the scene as a desert preacher preaching a message of repentance. His lifestyle was simple but radical. He wore clothes made from camel's hair, ate wild honey and locusts, and had a leather belt around his waist. Jesus said that he was the greatest man born of a woman this side of heaven. Paul spent some years in the wilderness of Arabia after his conversion. Though called to be an apostle to the Gentiles at his conversion, he was not yet ready for the task. God used him in a mighty way only after he spent fourteen years in the

---

7. Lane, *The Solace of Fierce Landscapes*, 53.

"wilderness". Jesus was also not spared of the desert as a training ground. He became famished and faint at the end of forty days in the desert. The angels came to minister to him after he overcame the temptations of the flesh. Throughout his ministry, Jesus often retreated to solitary places to be alone with God.

Like Abraham, Moses, David, John the Baptist, Paul, and even Jesus before us, we too need to take heed to the call of the desert. This call was proposed to me when I read Henri Nouwen's book, *The Way of the Heart*. I came across the spirituality of the Desert Fathers for the first time. In his book, the writer introduced me to the sayings of the Desert Fathers and the discipline of solitude and silence. The book spoke to my inner dissatisfaction and aroused in me a longing for authentic Christianity. I was in touch with a tradition outside my own for the first time.

The call was also echoed through my close affinity with mountains. Hoping to trek the Himalayas one day, I hang a picture of the Himalayan Mountains on the wall behind my desk in my office. The ruggedness of these majestic mountains challenges and inspires me. I love trekking the hills. Once a week, I walk up the steep trail that winds its way up to the top. I am practically breathless by the time I reach there but enjoying every moment of it. I love listening to the silence around me and to the crushing of fallen leaves under my tired feet. I will stop for a while at the top to warm down and continue on a deserted road that leads to another station. The road is less steep and level in some places, and I can relax my feet and leisurely enjoy my silent walk through a forest of trees untouched by human habitation.

A highlight of my life was when I climbed Mount Kinabalu, South East Asia's highest mountain. It is the most climbable mountain in its class at just over 4000 meters high. The experience was exhilarating and unforgettable. The tree-line ends at a certain height just below the pinnacle. Above the tree-line, the vast empty space of pure rocky terrain has a desert-like appearance. At the last stage of the hike, climbers need to begin the climb as early as 2 a.m. in the morning in order to reach the peak by 6 a.m. This is to ensure that the climbers will be able to witness the spectacular sight of the rising sun that slowly pierces, like a ball of fire, through the clouds below. The trek to the top on a cloudless, moonlight night gave me a surreal sensation. I felt I was on another planet. Reaching the top and looking down at the steep void that descended three thousand feet to the valley below sent a chill down my spine. I instinctively looked for the ropes and watched my steps carefully. My respect and awe for the mountains was renewed. I had written a poem to commemorate this mountain experience. It is entitled *The Climb to the Top*.

> Pins of light piercing the night/Inching up the incline on a hike/Moon, stars joined to give light/ To the top, the pilgrims' pride;
>
> Paused often to suck in air/Measured steps on rocks of stairs/Lungs gasping with little to spare/Breathless, a breathtaking stare;
>
> Playful mix of light and shadow/Gave the rocks-cape a surreal glow/Tearing the heavens in motion slow/The sun woke up for the day's show;
>
> The rock loomed large on the steep/At its tip, it dropped three thousand feet/ It tipped us not to yield to defeat/We tripped its spine with heavy feet;
>
> At Low's Peak, the feeling was high/Sent a chill down our aching spine/Attired for winter in a hot clime/Fists punched the chilly air in triumph.

The mountain, according to some people, symbolizes the dreamer's deep desire for transcendence—a longing and thirst for God. That is why the mountain carries a certain appeal and attraction to some people. Many mountain climbers share the experience that their climb is more than physical; there is a spiritual dimension to it. If one asks the climbers why they climb the mountain, their typical answer is that because it is there. This is not exactly true. It is not just about conquering a peak to prove a point. It is this longing for transcendence that draws them to the mountains. Through the ages, people who want to draw closer to God tend to build their abode high up and hidden away in the mountains.

Entering the Emptiness

This deep desire for transcendence also led man to build another kind of mountain in the twelve century. It was a man-made massive structure that rose above the landscape and dwarfed all the buildings around it at the time when it was built. The smart use of geometric dimensions and light make the Gothic cathedral a unique place of worship. The mathematical principles of symmetry and harmonious proportions are painstakingly applied to the design and structure of the building. Its cross-ribbed vault grows like branches of trees sprouting skyward which forms the roof of the cathedral. This gives the onlooker a sense of awe and wonder. The walls are no longer used to support the massive roof as in the older buildings. Pillars now support the roof instead. Large openings are punched along the thin walls to allow light to enter the building. Stained glass windows provide the luminous sense that God's grace is pouring into the sanctuary. The Gothic cathedral strives to make an earthly form of the heavenly image. It is a kind of celestial city on earth. Man does not need to go up a mountain to get a vision of God. He now needs to enter the Gothic cathedral to be transported to heaven.

Make Space for God

The call of the desert is a call to emptiness. The desert may be stingy on many things but not on empty space. Unlike the tropical forest that is cluttered with trees, bushes, and undergrowth, the desert has lots of spaces in between. Sue Monk Kidd makes this observation in her book, *God's Joyful Surprise*.[8] She calls us to consider the spaces that God has designed in the world. The spaces between trees give the forest its serenity. There will be no music if there are no spaces between the notes of a concerto or symphony. Words become meaningful when there are spaces between them. She recalls the time her daughter Ann was playing with the typewriter. She kept hitting the keys without touching

---

8. Kidd, *God's Joyful Surprise*, 161–62.

the space bar. The words all ran together that didn't make sense. Our life is just like that. We hardly hit the space bar. We must learn to make space for God to come in and make his home with us.

The workplace is the arena where we can easily succumbed to idolatry. It is the place where we feel most competent. We are able to exercise control at work by using our skills and strategies to perform a task. Sabbath is enacted by God as a space between periods of work. It is to remind us that we are not in control but God. God is in charge, and we need to trust him that he will keep the world moving even when he decides to take a day off. If we are not careful, our work can be an idol. Sabbath-keeping makes sure that this doesn't happen. To Eugene Peterson, Sabbath-keeping is our weekly housecleaning. It is to begin the week uncluttered with idols. It is to detach ourselves from the world's way of doing things which usually compels us to take things into our own hands.[9]

The way to make space for God is to empty ourselves. Mirroring the outer landscape, our interior landscape needs to be purged of the false self in order for the true self to be resurrected. The desert provides an excellent environment for the death of self. By definition, a desert is an arid region where rainfall is less than ten inches per annum. They average less than half an inch per year in some places and in parts of the Sahara, there is not even any rainfall for more than twenty years. The rain water, in such places, evaporates before it reaches the ground. The temperature at ground level can reach up to two hundred degrees Fahrenheit. The wind, at such heat, can cause the human body to lose moisture as much as a quart per hour.[10] In a place where nothing grows and human existence is under threat from the harsh elements, God has found the perfect place to do his acts of salvation. We need to die in order to be resurrected. When Jesus spoke of his death he reminded his audience about a kernel of

9. Peterson, *Christ Plays in Ten Thousands Places*, 128–9.
10. Lane, *Solace of Fierce Landscapes*, 38.

wheat falling to the ground. If it doesn't die it will remain a single seed; if it does it will produce many seeds. New life springs up when death occurs. One way to empty ourselves is the abandonment of control. The desert is clever in doing that. The silence and solitude one encounters in the desert will lead the traveler to the abandonment of self.

Abandonment of Language

Julian of Norwich suddenly became ill for three days when she was thirty years old. She lost her ability to speak, and her sight slowly failed her. She was given up dead, and the last rites were administered to her. During this time when she was in utter silence and losing control of her life, she went through an extraordinary experience that impacted her for the rest of her life. She explained what had happened after the near death experience. She felt that she was "nothing" when her life was being emptied and her ability to speak and exist was stripped away. Later she would teach about the poverty of self made aware by the utter impotence in silent prayer. Language is often used as an agent of control. We use words to manipulate, influence, and propagate. We feel a sense of losing control without the use of words. No wonder silence is painful and unbearable for many of us.

Some years ago, I asked students and faculty to observe four hours of complete silence at a retreat. Some of them could not keep still after a while. They began to occupy their minds with some physical or mental activity. A couple of students went to dip themselves at a nearby spring. Another person picked pebbles and threw them aimlessly into the flowing stream. One student was busy watching a trail of ants on a rock. One was tempted to sing. Another picked up a guitar pretending to strum the strings. Most of them needed to do something to release the nervous energy. Almost all of them looked forward for the time of silence to end. During sharing, students talked about their frustrations for not doing anything at all. They felt useless and guilty about wasting their time. Not able to talk with friends for an extended time, even though they were close by, could be an anguished experience. I do not blame them. Students live in a milieu where words are used all the time. They live in a wordy world. They listen to teachers teaching, preachers preaching, and students presenting reports all day long. Words and more words are used all the time. Henri Nouwen points this out:

> They are caught in such a complex network of discussions, debates, and arguments about God and "God-issues" that a simple conversation with God or a simple presence to God has become practically impossible . . . if there is a crisis in theological education; it is first and foremost a crisis of the word.[11]

Abandonment of Self

We not only die to our speech in the desert but we also die to our self as well. We soon find out that the desert ignores our presence totally. To Edward Abbey, author and radical environmentalist, this is the desert's gift to us:

> The finest quality of these stones, these plants and animals, this desert landscape is the indifference manifest to our presence, our absence, our coming, our staying or our going. Whether we live or die, is a matter of absolutely no concern whatsoever to the desert.[12]

Like Job, our world may come crashing down and falling into pieces. We feel the pain, bear the sorrows, and cry out in bitterness. Yet God, like the desert, is indifferent to our pain. Our confidence, hope, faith, imagination, intelligence, and feelings are stripped away, and we feel emptiness inside us. This nothingness reflects the empty spaces of the desert. Out of nothingness,

---

11. Nouwen, *Way of the Heart*, 47.
12. Abbey, *Desert Solitare*, 267.

the self abandons itself to God. Meister Eckhart has this to say about abandonment.

> If we want to live and want your works to live, you must be dead to all things and have become nothing. It is characteristic of creatures that they make something out of something, while it is characteristic of God that he makes something out of nothing. Therefore, if God is to make anything in you or with you, you must first have become nothing.[13]

I remember the time when I was with my wife at the doctor's office. Earlier she went to a neighborhood clinic and was told that she had gastric. The doctor prescribed some medication, but it did not help the bloating in her stomach. Finally we decided to see a doctor we knew. The doctor gave her a scan of the affected area. We did not expect anything suspicious at all. The result of the scan came as a shock when the doctor broke the bad news to us. My wife had ovarian cancer. We were speechless—numbed by shock. We did not know how to respond to this sudden news. The world that we had carefully constructed over the years came crashing down on us like a pile of bricks. We found ourselves transported to a place of desolation. We felt abandoned and left alone in a vast, empty space. Metaphorically speaking, we had entered a desert without our knowledge. We began to slowly pick up the pieces again through the long, anxious months of visiting hospitals and cancer therapy. Life after the crisis was never the same. Stripped bare and empty, we had developed a new way of looking at the world and at ourselves. The desert's indifference is a gift of God to us. God is able to do something in us only when we have been abandoned and become nothing.

---

13. Cited by Lane, *Solace of Fierce Landscapes*, 76. See Eckhart, "German Sermon 39," 296–7.

Being Truly Human

Abandonment of Neighbor

The desert also teaches us to die to the neighbor. We tend to view ourselves through the lens of others. The expectations and perceptions of others greatly concern us. We crave for the approval and applause of significant others in our life. Losing their approval leads us to despair and discouragement. The compulsive preoccupation with what others think of us means that we are dealing with a self-image that needs constant mending. The desert, on the other hand, is indifferent to all this panting for attention. This is the gift of the desert to us. There is no gallery for the false self to play to in the desert. There is no audience. All is emptiness. With no one to applaud or criticize us, we are free to be ourselves without fear of misunderstanding and prejudice.

One day a brother came to see Abba Macarius who was the abbot of the monastery at Scetis. He came to ask the abbot how to be holy. The abbot told the brother to go to a nearby cemetery to abuse the dead. "Curse them with all your might and even throw stones," he told him. The brother went and did as instructed. When he came back the abbot asked him, "What did the dead say to you?" "Nothing," the younger monk replied. The older monk then asked him to go back to the same place again, but this time heap praises on them even calling them apostles, saints, and righteous men. The brother did as told. "Did the dead say anything when you praise them?" the older man asked. "Nothing," the brother replied, "They still did not answer to either my curses or praises." "Ah they must be holy people," remarked Abba Macarius. "You insulted them, and they did not reply you; you praised them, and they did not say anything. Go and do likewise, just as the dead." This is how the desert teaches one to die to one's neighbor.[14]

We are free to be ourselves when we die to our neighbor. We have dismantled the scaffolding of our false self. We no longer care about how or what people think of us because we do not subject our lives to the dictates of others. As Paul, in his letter

---

14. Ward, *The Sayings of the Desert Fathers*, 132.

to the Corinthians, points out that a man's conscience is clear, for he neither cares on how people judge him nor does he judge himself.[15] Take the example of Abba Moses. A magistrate in the city was keen to meet Abba Moses, for he heard that he was a devout person. He came to the desert with the aim to search for him. When he met the first person, he asked to see the father. The man told the magistrate not to waste time looking for the monk, for he would be disappointed. He quietly whispered to him that this Abba Moses was a fraud and a heretic. He was not what people said he was. He urged the magistrate not to search further but to return home. This new revelation deeply disappointed him. The magistrate returned home to his friends and relatives keen to bring down the reputation of this monk. Then someone asked him to describe exactly the person he met. "Was it by chance a tall black man?" he asked. The magistrate replied in the affirmative. He was told that the man he first met was indeed Abba Moses. The magistrate went away greatly edified.[16]

The Desert Fathers fled to the desert to seek God and to deal with their false self. The desert milieu provides an ideal place to deal with the compulsions of life. In the desert, life is simple—a stone hut with a roof of branches over it, a mat for bed, a sheepskin to keep warm, a jar of water to quench thirst, and a lamp to give light. Sleep is kept at a minimum, and a meal a day is the norm. This simple, uncluttered life helps them to be attentive in seeking after God. Prayer orientates their entire life (body, mind, and spirit) to God. Solitude and silence set the conditions necessary for prayer. This does not mean that there are no temptations in the desert. The outward temptations of the world have now turned inward. The world went with them into the wilderness. The world within their hearts was even harder to deal than the outside world. The greatest fear of the Fathers was not the external world they left behind, but the world and the false self they carried within them.

15. 1 Cor 4:3.
16. Ward, *The Sayings*, 140.

The Deserts of our Life

Do we literally need to enter a desert in order to get rid of the false self? Many of us who live in the tropics have not seen a real desert in all our life. On the other hand, we can carve out a "desert" for ourselves. The discipline of solitude and silence will help us to create a wilderness in the soul. The interior desert in us mirrors the exterior desert with its harsh conditions and empty spaces. I will write about this discipline in the next chapter. Like Julian of Norwich, we can enter a desert involuntarily when faced with an illness, loss, or crisis in our life.

My younger brother died of cancer last year. We were at his ward daily visiting and attending to his needs. He had bedsores on his back that was so big that one could literally put a fist in it. Fortunately, the cancer had spread to his neck causing paralysis to the bottom half of his body. He felt no pain. Three patients had died in the same ward during the two weeks we were there. Death stared at us with a scorn. The hospital attendants unceremoniously and quietly put away the bodies. A sense of loss and numbness filled the air. Patients and nurses went about doing the routine chores as if nothing had happened. Life on the surface looked normal. We tend to hide our fears in the midst of loss. Perhaps our preoccupation outwardly is one way to cope with the emptiness inside us. Then one early morning I received a call from the hospital. It was an emergency, and I needed to come to attend to my brother immediately. He was dying. The last hour before he passed away, I was holding his cold hand and feeling his weakening pulse. I whispered into his ear to tell him to let go of his frail life, and let God bring him home. During the final moments, we hummed and sang the song, *Amazing Grace*, at his bedside. It was a beautiful moment to say goodbye. He died peacefully without struggle. For the past two weeks, I went through a desert in my life. I came out of it with a deeper sense of my own vulnerability and humanness. I was surprised that I came out of this experience feeling renewed and strengthened. I was glad and thankful to God that my brother could finally head home after two years of struggle with cancer.

The desert has its surprises for us. It is not only a place of death but of resurrection also. The prophet Isaiah paints the desert as a parched land—a thirsty ground of burning sand. It saps the strength of those who dare to enter it. Yet transformation takes place when the emptied and abandoned soul yields itself to its fierce winds. Water begins to gush out and steams flow in the desert causing the desert to bloom. When the desert blooms, it is a delight and joy to see the dramatic change from ugliness to beauty, desolation to joy, and fatigue to renewed energy. The prophet Isaiah penned these words:

> The desert and the parched land will be glad; the wilderness will rejoice and blossom. Like crocus, it will burst into bloom; it will rejoice greatly and shout for joy. The glory of Lebanon will be given to it, the splendor of Carmel and Sharon; they will see the glory of the Lord, the splendor of God.[17]

There is yet another way for us to enter a desert in our life. The desert can be anywhere where the familiar structures of the world have fallen apart—a desolated place filled with despair and little hope. It is an empty wasteland, forsaken and ignored by the world, where few people want to venture into it. An aids hospital, a hospice for terminally ill patients, a mental asylum, a center for the intellectually disabled children, a nursing home for the elderly and infirmed, a counseling center for abused women and children, a drug rehab center for addicts can become a desert for us. In these desolated places, we learn to embrace the pain and suffering of the residents and share the solidarity of abandonment and nothingness with them. If we do that, we have carved out a "desert" for ourselves without entering a physical desert.

We face different kinds of "deserts" in our life. According to James Houston, my professor at Regent College, there is more

17. Isa 35:1–2.

than one kind of desert experience. Each personality with their personal stories will face a different kind of desert experience. For example, the "perfectionist" will face a desert of imperfection. God will expose his weakness and give him the humility to work through them. The "giver" will face the desert of inadequacy. In times of trouble, he is hard-pressed to seek help from others and God. The "doer" will face a desert of uselessness. He finds himself to be going nowhere and powerless to solve the situation he faces. The "idealist" will confront a desert of ordinariness. He finds life routine, bored, and lacking creativity. A desert of flux and disorientation is given to the "rigid" that is afraid of change. The "fun-lover" will be transported to a desert place of pain and suffering to sober him down. The "controller" will face a desert of chaos and uncertainty and the desert will challenge the "pleaser" to confront reality and stand up to the truth.[18]

Desert Detours

God did not take the northern route which was the shorter way to Canaan when he led Israel out of Egypt to the Promised Land. Instead, Israel had to make a detour through the Sinai desert using a longer and more challenging route. The desert seems to be God's preferred way to train God's people for a rugged faith hardened by the wild terrain and fierce desert winds. God knew that Israel needed to have a strong faith in order to survive spiritually in Canaan—a land infested with idols. Besides, Israel had been exposed to the idols in Egypt for too long. Hopefully the desert would just be the place of purgation.

Mark's Gospel begins with John the Baptist calling people to repentance in the desert. John was such a charismatic prophet of God that the whole Judean countryside and those from Jerusalem came to him. He wore clothing made from camel's hair and had a leather belt around his waist. He ate locusts and wild

---

18. Houston, *The Heart's Desire*, 178.

honey. Jesus, like the rest, also came to John in the wilderness to be baptized. John pointed others to Jesus and called him the Lamb of God who would take away the sins of the world. We would expect Jesus, in view of John's testimony, to begin his ministry of preaching and healing straightaway. Instead he needed to take a detour. The Holy Spirit literally propelled him into the desert for forty days. Jesus knew the importance of taking detours to the isolated places. Mark records for us that it was his habit to go to a solitary place early in the morning when it was dark to be alone with God.[19]

Moses too took a detour to the desert. When standing up for his own people, he killed an Egyptian for beating a fellow Hebrew. Afraid that Pharaoh would kill him for what he did, he ran to the desert to save his skin. He spent forty years tending sheep in the wilderness in a place not too far from Mount Sinai, the mountain of God. So was David. Though anointed king of Israel by the prophet Samuel, he had to wait for his time to come. Meanwhile David had to flee from King Saul who, out of jealousy and hate, was bent on finding and killing him. David and his men spent considerable time in the desert to avoid detection from Saul's men.

Desert detours are good for the soul. "We need the tonic of wildness," writes H. D. Thoreau.[20] We may not need to wait for God to detour us to a desert place. We can detour daily to a solitary place to pray in solitude and silence. One day a monk asked Abba Moses for a word. "Go and sit in your cell and your cell will teach you everything," he said.[21] The monk, when confined to a time of silence and solitude in the cell, would open a space in his heart for God to teach him the way of the desert. Blaise Pascal once wrote that all the unhappiness of men arises from one single fact: they cannot stay quietly in their own room.[22]

19. Mark 1:35.
20. Thoreau, *Walden*, 265.
21. Ward, *The Sayings of the Desert Fathers*, 139.
22. Pascal, *Pensees*, 42.

These desert detours are needful for those who are at the forefront of ministering to others in Christ's Name. In his celebrated book, *The Way of the Heart*, Henri Nouwen points out that the pressures in the ministry are enormous, the demands are increasing, and the satisfaction diminishing. He then asks these questions:

> How can we expect to remain full of creative vitality, of zeal for the Word of God, of desire to serve, and of motivation to inspire our often numbed congregations? Where are we supposed to find nurture and strength? How can we alleviate our own spiritual hunger and thirst?

For an answer to these questions, Nouwen looks to the Desert Fathers for inspiration. He concludes:

> By their solitude, silence, and unceasing prayer the Desert Fathers show us the way. These disciplines will teach us to stand firm, to speak words of salvation, and to approach the new millennium with hope, courage, and confidence.[23]

Questions to Consider and Reflect

1. Do you entertain idols in your heart that confine and reduce God to a concept, an experience, ongoing projects or a set of rules?

2. Were you abandoned by God before? Were there times when God seemed distant and your confidence, hope, faith, and trust taken from you and you became "nothing."?

3. Are you the type who is conscious of what people think of you? Do you constantly seek the approval of significant others in your life? Have you ever wondered why you behave in this way?

---

23. Nouwen, *Way of the Heart*, 12–3, 94.

Chapter 3

Solitude and Silence

In solitude one is never alone.
The spirit was not made for noise, but for taking things in.
Life is a preparation for heaven,
 not only through deserving work,
 but by the peace and communion with God.
But mankind throws itself into infinite discussions.
The little good he finds in noise should prove
 how far he has strayed from his vocation.

—CHARLES FOUCAULD[1]

Go and Sit in Your Cell

ONE DAY, AN ELDERLY person came to Archbishop Anthony Bloom to see him about her prayer life. After some discussion, the bishop told her that if she spoke all the time she would not give God a chance to put a word to her. He recommended that she go to a room, quietly settle down on an armchair, knit for fifteen minutes before the face of God, and enjoy the peace of the place. She did not think it was a very pious advice. How could sitting alone for fifteen minutes help with her prayer life? Nevertheless

---

1. Foucauld, *Charles De Foucauld*, 82.

she went ahead and did what the bishop told her. Later she came back excited about what she had gone through. "It works," she told him. The bishop was curious too and asked, "What works?" She told him of her experience:

> And I became more and more aware of the silence. The needles hit the armrest of my chair, the clock was ticking peacefully, there was nothing to bother about, I had no need of straining myself, and then I perceived that this silence was not simply an absence of noise, but that the silence had substance. It was not absence of something but presence of something. The silence had a density, a richness, and it began to pervade me. The silence around began to come and meet the silence in me. All of a sudden I perceived that the silence was a presence. At the heart of the silence there was He who is all stillness, all peace, all poise.[2]

Once someone asked Abba Anthony what it took to please God. The old man told him to take note of three things: "Whoever you may be, always have God before your eyes; whatever you do, do it according to the testimony of the Holy Scriptures; in whatever place you live, do not easily leave it."[3]

The first two advices seem logical and sound reasonable. The third advice sounds a bit out of place in today's world of hurry and high mobility. Do we need to stay put in one place as long as we can? The fact that this was mentioned clearly showed that staying put in one place was already a problem for some people in the days of Abba Anthony. To stay put in the cell, in solitude and silence, for an extended time can be a challenge for most of us today. We need patience which is lacking in an age of instantaneous gratification.

The machines that make things convenient and efficient for us also shape us to be impatient. The car is a good example. It

---

2. Cited by Gorsuch, *An Invitation to the Spiritual Journey*, 83. See Bloom, *Beginning to Pray*, 49.

3. Ward, *The Sayings of the Desert Fathers*, 2.

can take us to places in a breeze. Most city folks cannot imagine living without having a car. Car rage is also common among city motorists. Our impatience towards other motorists surprises us especially during rush hour. We easily get agitated driving behind a slow moving vehicle. We blow the horn to signal our impatience, and inconsiderate motorists will get a mouthful from us. Finding a parking lot and be the first to claim it can be a challenge. The crowded car park turns into a concrete jungle. At the sight of an empty spot, our beastly instincts tell us that we need to get aggressive and be there first before others lay claim on it.

The other modern invention is the supermarket—a one-stop shopping under one roof. The modern supermarket is a convenient place to shop. The place is designed with the customer in mind. Products are stacked along wide aisles and neat rows for easy, comfortable shopping. One of the frustrations that I have is to queue in line at the cash counter. My impatience is getting at me when I am done with my shopping and heading to the cash counter. I scan the lines at the different counters and mentally take note of that one line that has less people with shopping carts that are not filled to the brim. I quickly claim the spot behind the queue and patiently wait for my turn. Sometimes the shortest line may end up taking the longest to clear! Regretting that I have chosen the wrong line adds to my frustration.

An Inner World of Chaos

The practice of solitude and silence is a challenge for us who live in an age of hurry. We lack the patience to sit still in the cell for long. An inner world of chaos opens up in us the moment we shut the outer world of noise and people behind us. Shutting the door behind us does not mean that we have gotten rid of the world. We carry the world into our solitude and silence. We give up the practice easily when distracted by all these noises and thoughts in our head. We want to get busy again so that it can shield us from the inner chaos. It is difficult to be alone because the inner thoughts of feelings, fantasies, ideas, memories, and desires are like the wild beasts that keep assaulting us. They keep knocking at our mind's door and will not leave us alone. At times when I read the Gospel of Mark, I wonder why the apostle makes this remark that the wild animals were with Jesus when he was alone spending forty days with God in the desert.[4] Now I can understand the significance of it.

How to get rid of the wild thoughts and feelings that keep knocking at our mind's door? The trick is not to pay attention to them. We must not fight against these intruding thoughts and feelings. We acknowledge their existence and let them pass by. Suppose a familiar face passes by when I am in deep conversation with another person. I acknowledge her presence with a nod and continue to talk to my friend. The knocking, after some time, will diminish if I do not open the door to let in the visitors. Unwelcomed the visitors will slowly fade away. The knocking becomes less, but it will not go away altogether. We can only reap its benefits if we persevere to stay put in the cell.

Giving God our Undivided Attention

The discipline of solitude and silence is not a time and place for us to enjoy some privacy away from the intrusions of the world, or for us to recharge or refresh ourselves after a period of stressful work or personal loss. It is not to escape from people and responsibilities, or to give ourselves some space to think, reflect, or do the things that we like. All these are helpful and have their places in our lives. We should set aside time for recreation, reflection, and recharging our worn-out batteries. The discipline of solitude and silence is different. It is to open a space in our cluttered life for God to make a home in us. In this space, God has our undivided attention without us setting any agenda or control.

---

4. Mark 1:13.

There is no one correct or best way to observe this discipline. Each person is different in temperament and personality and has to find her own niche in it. Nevertheless, for those who want to grow in this discipline, certain guidelines need to be observed. First of all, we must be committed to exercising this discipline on a regular basis. We will not reap any benefit out of it if we do it on an ad-hoc or inconsistent basis. Rhythm and flow are critical to the progress of any spiritual discipline. We need to do it at least once a day. It is also essential that we practice this discipline at a familiar place and fixed time. Changing places and time often will disrupt the rhythm and flow needful for growth in the discipline.

The place must be free from all kinds of distractions. A room or space cluttered with things is not conducive because it reminds us of unfinished tasks that need attention. If we do not have the luxury to afford an uncluttered space, we can do our solitude and silence early in the morning when the place is still dark. In this way, we will not notice the things around us. The place must also be free from all sources of unwelcomed noises coming from the phone, radio, and television. God alone will have our attention in solitude and silence.

The place must be well-ventilated with a good flow of fresh air so that we can stay alert. The air temperature is also important because too cold or too warm will bring discomfort to the physical condition. Make sure that the spot we choose to settle down for the discipline is comfortable but not too comfortable to our body. Sleep and drowsiness may be induced by a comfortable spot. Any physical discomfort caused by the environment can be a distraction and a hindrance to the practice of solitude and silence. We may need to experiment with various spots in the house to get the optimal space for our discipline. We try to stick to it as long as we can once we have decided on a spot.

The posture should keep us alert at all times. We need to experiment with various postures and choose one that is optimal to the discipline. A posture that will keep us alert and not induce us to sleep or feel lazy is the right one. I find that kneeling with my back straight and a pillow underneath or between my legs will keep me comfortable and alert at the same time. We should also pay attention to the breathing. Deep, correct breathing will help the body to relax and the mind to be attentive.

How long should we spend in solitude and silence? We should begin in small steps. A few minutes at the beginning are sufficient. As we progress, we can increase the time to about twenty minutes or half an hour a day. Time passes quickly when we get deeper into the practice of solitude and silence. It is good to end this time by praying the Lord's Prayer aloud. We may want to continue this time with verbalized prayer, praise, and petitions to God.

The Use of the Prayer Word

We should not have any expectations when we enter into this time of silent prayer. To expect something is to orientate the mind or thoughts on something other than God. Our attention, or rather our intention, should be on God and not on our thoughts, feelings, or concepts. We should reach God with pure faith. It is not easy to let go of our thoughts to reach God with pure faith. Hence we need something else to center ourselves. We need a prayer-word that redirects the intention of opening up ourselves to God and to his presence. The meaning of the prayer-word is not important. The use of the prayer-word is to express our intention or desire for God. A prayer-word like "Jesus," "Father," or "Lord, have mercy" can be used to express the willingness to come before him uninhibited by any personal agenda or striving.[5]

We simply come to God by opening ourselves to him. We must not feel agitated or distracted when unwelcomed thoughts come knocking at our mind's door. We acknowledge their presence and let them go. If these thoughts keep coming in waves,

---

5. For an excellent introduction to this type of silent prayer, see Keating's *Open Mind, Open Heart*.

we can use the prayer-word to redirect our attention to God. We may have to use the prayer-word and repeating it often to deal with the relentless flow of thoughts assaulting the mind at the beginning. Through time and much practice, we will find ourselves using the prayer-word less often. Eventually we may not need to use it at all.

We should not judge or expect something out of this period of solitude and silence. We may feel that nothing has happened, and we are wasting our time. Later we will see the results outside of our prayer life. We need to be patient and persevere in this discipline before we can reap the benefits. Gradually we find ourselves more at ease, more confident, less fearful or anxious. Something has changed inside us without our knowledge. Thomas Keating, in his bestselling book, *Open Mind, Open Heart*, has this to say:

> In this prayer God is speaking not to your ears, to your emotions, or to your head, but to your spirit, to your inmost being. There is no human apparatus to understand the language or to hear it. A kind of anointing takes place. The fruits of that anointing will appear later in ways that are indirect: in your calmness, in your peace, in your willingness to surrender to God in everything that happens.[6]

The Source of our Confidence

I entered into a time of solitude by chance when I was forced to spend a period of several days alone by myself. I stayed in my mum's apartment in Penang due to unforeseen circumstances. I had the whole apartment to myself because the place was empty. There was nothing much in the house to keep me occupied. I read the daily newspaper, Bible, and some books I brought along with me in order to kill time. I resisted going out; I had to watch

---

6. Keating, *Open Mind, Open Heart*, 83.

my spending carefully because my funds were low. I hardly spoke to anyone and saw anybody during the ten days of solitary confinement. I was counting my days hoping to return back to Singapore. I did not think much about my solitary confinement after I left Penang. I was just glad that I could finally get out of the house. It was some time later that I noticed a subtle change in me. I became more assured, more calm and free, and was no longer afflicted with the need to prove myself before others. Gradually I was back to my old self again when the effects slowly wore off.

I can relate to David in Psalm 27 when recalling this incident. In the first three verses, David is saying that he has no fear of his enemies. Apparently he is under attack by an army that aims to cut him down. He writes, "Though war break out against me, even then I will be confident." Where is the source of David's confidence? Verse 4 is the answer. David says that the one thing he needs, in times like this, is to seek the Lord's presence with the purpose "to gaze upon the beauty of the Lord and to seek him in the temple." David does not enter God's presence to petition the Lord immediately to save him from his enemies. His prayer for help begins in verse 7 through to verse 12. David ends the psalm in verses 13 and 14 again affirming his confidence that he will personally witness the Lord's goodness in his life. This psalm reminds us that David's confidence, when faced with fear, is the direct result of his time spent in silent prayer and adoration before God. There he spends time gazing on God and desiring his presence. While leaving his problems behind him, he sets his heart waiting on God. It is only after spending time with God, in solitude and silence, that David begins his prayer to God to vindicate him before his enemies. He calls out to God in verse 7, "Hear my voice when I call, O Lord; be merciful to me and answer me."

Prayer of the Mind

From this psalm, we gather that it is out of solitude and silence that prayer is practiced. Usually this is not the case. We go to God in prayer with the mind overflowing with words and ideas. Just like the disciples on the road to Emmaus, we lack interior silence. The disciples' minds were working overtime trying to figure out what had happened earlier in Jerusalem. The event of Jesus' sudden death gripped their attention and became the topic of intense debate and discussion. There was too much noise between the ears that kept them from recognizing and responding to Jesus. The mind can be a hindrance to our prayer life because the intellect is used to master the world, while we need to relinquish control in prayer.

Once I heard a pastor sharing from the pulpit concerning a church member who had difficulty praying. She told the pastor that, at times, she could not find any words to pray to God. She had exhausted her prayer vocabulary and was struggling to find the right words to speak. While praying she found herself repeating the same words all over again. Why is prayer so difficult for many of us? Prayer, for some of us, is like a one-way conversation and all we hear is our own voice. We often wonder whether God listens to our prayers at all. We are naturally frustrated if prayer is purely talking to God because when we talk we expect some feedback or response.

Why do we always associate prayer with speech? Speech and thinking engages the mind more than the heart. Talking and thinking are ways where the mind is most engaged. Perhaps this is the reason we find it tough to remain silent. We want to fill the "empty space" with words and thoughts. We use speech to fill the exterior silence and thoughts to fill the interior silence. Can speech and thoughts be hindrances to our prayer life? The answer is yes. We can use speech and thoughts to gain mastery over our prayer life if we are not careful. Robert Warren in his book, *The Practice of Prayer*, warns about too much prayer that can harm one's spiritual health. He admits that it is a strange way to end his book on prayer with such a warning:

> Our problem stems from living in a self-centered, technological society addicted to taking control . . . Take that mentality into prayer, and we will be in trouble, for to assume that our prayer life is primarily dependent on us is what will seriously damage our knowledge of God.[7]

In Matthew 7:7, Jesus says that if we ask, it will be given to us; seek and we will find; knock and the door will be opened to us. We need to use words when we ask for something. When we seek, we will talk less than when we ask for something. When we search for something or someone, we may occasionally ask about the whereabouts of the thing or person we look for. We usually will not speak when we knock on the door. We pause in silence for the person in the room to respond to our knock by opening the door for us. This progression in prayer from speech to silence is noted by Soren Kierkegaard, a Danish philosopher and theologian. He writes, "A man prayed, and at first he thought that prayer was talking. But he became more and more quiet until he realized that prayer is listening."[8] We should not feel frustrated when we have no more words to speak. We should learn to yield our words to God and allow the heart to take over. One way to overcome this difficulty is to see prayer not so much a communication of ideas but a communion of presence. Carlo Carretto has this interesting point to make:

> Prayer is like love. Words pour at first. Then we are more silent and can communicate in monosyllables. In difficulties a gesture is enough, a word, or nothing at all—love is enough . . . The soul converses with God with a single loving glance.[9]

---

7. Warren, *The Practice of Prayer*, 190.
8. Kierkegaard, *Christian Discourses*, 324.
9. Carretto, *Letters from the Desert*, 46.

The Power of Silence

I remember those times when I was at a loss for words. I had difficulty talking to someone who had just lost a loved one. I was sent there to give consolation, and I struggled using the right words to console a grieving person. I knew that I had to say something, and I was searching hard in my mind what to say in a situation like this. The words that came out might sound nice, comforting, and even pastoral, but it did not touch the heart. They sounded hollow, shallow, and superficial. It was mind-talk. Sometimes a better option is to feel and share grief with the other person in silence. It is better not to say anything at all if we cannot find words to say. Shared silence is better than careless speech. To Belden Lane, the power of silence can connect and heal:

> As our guests arrived later in the week, I was curious to notice how we related to each other in this common observance of silence . . . We smiled and nodded in passing, but refrained from small talk and niceties ordinarily expected in polite society. As a result, something unusual began to occur. Instead of ignoring these people, I found myself oddly caring for them, valuing their presence without even knowing their names. I started praying for them during the offices, looking forward to their being present even when nothing apparently passed between us. I'd never related to other people in such a way, connected by nothing more than a deliberate silence.[10]

There is a place for verbal or mental prayer. Speaking to God and thinking about God are legitimate ways of praying, but prayer is more than the activity of the mind. It involves the heart as well. It is possible that our mind is full of talk and thoughts when we pray, but our heart is empty and far away from God. Words coming from an empty heart sound hollow like the sound of gongs or cymbals. When we speak words out of a full heart filled with divine silence, they can be powerful and have far reaching consequences. God spoke to create a world of animate

---

10. Lane, *Solace of Fierce Landscapes*, 223.

and inanimate objects out of silence. After a time of solitude and silence, we do not need to say much when we pray. "Much can be said without much being spoken," writes Nouwen.[11] One day someone asked Abba Macarius how one should pray. The old saint said:

> There is no need at all to make long discourses; it is enough to stretch out one's hands and say, "Lord, as you will, and as you know, have mercy." And if the conflict grows fiercer say, "Lord, help!" He knows very well what we need and he shows us his mercy.[12]

The Night of the Soul

Those of us who seriously take up the practice of heart prayer need to know that, at some point, we will experience what John of the Cross describes as "the dark night of the soul." This "dark night" will make us feel that we have hit a dead end in the journey. We find ourselves entering a dry patch and nothing seems to excite us anymore. We lose the passion and appetite for the things in the world and for God. A sense of failure sinks in and to quit the inward journey becomes a temptation. The initial euphoria has subsided and it left behind a bitter taste. We may even be tempted to look elsewhere for another new spiritual adventure. John of the Cross explains that it is by divine appointment that we enter into the dark night, for God is using this time out of sheer grace to do a divine work in us. It is not a time to be fretful. Rather, it is a time for us to still the soul before God and wait patiently for the period to come to a close at God's own timing. Richard Foster comments that this dark night is like an operation that requires the patient to undergo anesthesia in order for the surgeon to perform the surgery successfully.[13]

---

11. Nouwen, *Way of the Heart*, 57.
12. Ward, *The Sayings of the Desert Fathers*, 131.
13. Foster, *Celebration of Discipline*, 128.

Solitude and Silence

What has happened is that we are going through a transitional period in our spiritual life. Like all transitions, we find ourselves confused, disorientated, and lost. I remember when I was in Hong Kong using the subway for the first time. The place was crowded with people moving in all directions. Even though I could read the signs in front of me, I was momentarily disorientated by the new place. It took me some time to figure out where to go and what to do. The dark night is like that of the birth of a child. She has to leave the warmth and security of the mother's womb, transit through the dark birth canal, before she exits into the bright world outside. Transitions should be welcomed because they are necessary for growth and progress. When we come out of the dark night, we will find that we are closer to the Kingdom of Heaven. John of the Cross, a sixteenth century Carmelite friar and priest, has these encouraging words for those of us who enter into the dark night.

> Oh, then, spiritual soul, when you see your appetites darkened, your inclinations dry and constrained, your faculties incapacitated for any interior exercise, do not be afflicted; think of this as a grace, since God is freeing you from yourself and taking you from your own activity.[14]

To the prophet Isaiah, this experience of the dark night is common to the saints of God. He writes: "Who among you fear the Lord and obeys the word of his servant? Let him who walks in the dark, who has no light, trust in the name of the Lord and rely on God."[15]

The Gift of Indifference

When a person is lost in a desert, he needs to value two important things in order to survive. First, he must not panic and be indifferent to the pain and despair that plague his mind. Second,

---

14. John of the Cross, *The Collected Works of St. John of the Cross*, 365.
15. Isa 50:10.

he needs to pay close attention to the surrounding to look for anything that may help to prolong his life. These two qualities, indifference and attentiveness, are fundamental to the desert way of spirituality. Belden Lane writes: "These two virtues are honed by exposure to the desert elements. The threat of the desert landscape has a way of eliciting the sharp, lean qualities of attentiveness and indifference."[16]

Normally, when we hit an empty spot in our life, we want to take control and give our full attention to it. Like air that cannot stand a vacuum, we want to fill the empty space as quickly as we possibly can. Strangely, the abandonment we experience in solitude and silence helps us to develop an attitude of indifference so that the urgent things in life become less urgent. We become less ruffled and no longer resisting to the emptiness inside us. We feel the pain without trying desperately to fix it. An indifference that "makes possible a lighter touch on everything, I'd considered important," writes Belden Lane.[17]

When my eldest daughter was in college in the United States, we face some difficulties financing her studies. We toyed with different options to finance her education. One obvious option was to get a bank loan. Another option was to borrow from friends or relatives. Since we did not like to be in debt, we decided to sell our house to pay for the costs. It was a tough decision. We were not able to sell the house right away because the property market was soft. Nothing happened when we prayed to God for him to open a way. It seemed that God was hidden and indifferent to our cry for help. Meanwhile we were desperate when no solution was in sight. After some struggle, I began to notice that something happened inside me. I was at peace even though the problem had not been solved. I was no longer concerned that our house should be sold immediately even though the bills kept mounting. I left the matter to God. As Lane points out, I had put a lighter touch on the matter that was previously screaming its head off

---

16. Lane, *Solace of Fierce Landscapes*, 188.
17. Lane, *Solace*, 58.

for my attention. The financial situation still gave me pain, but I had learned not to fight against it. Instead I felt the pain without trying to fix it. I had learnt to be indifferent to the compulsions that nagged at me.

The Gift of Attentiveness

The desert, by virtue of its sparse emptiness, offers little to distract us. The skills at observation are sharpened when honed by the desert environment. The senses are enhanced because our survival depends on them. Things that normally escape us in normal circumstances will attract our attention in the desert. The stars seem brighter and sharper at night; the silence has substance and depth; the shadows more alive and threatening. We tend to notice things better when we move at a slow pace. There is no hurry in the desert. When the pace of life slows down we begin to see things around us for the very first time.

One day I was walking with my students to the retreat hideout. Instead of taking the tram car to the top of Penang Hill, we decided to take a slow walk up the hill where the bungalow was. I did not expect the trip to take so much time. I was getting slightly impatient. A member of our group took her sweet time to pause and take notice of the things along the way. She was taking her time to enjoy the sights and sounds of the forest trail. I was anxious about reaching the destination on time. She sensed my impatience and made this remark, "It is not the destination but the journey that makes it worthwhile." I got the message. We often pay scant attention to the things that happen around us when in a hurry to go somewhere.

In her essay, *Reflections on the Right Use of School Studies with a view to the Love of God,* Simone Weil stresses on the need for Christians to understand that the sole object of studies is to develop the faculty of attention. She defines attention as "suspending our thought, leaving it detached, empty, and ready to be penetrated by the object." According to her, school studies are effective in increasing the power of attention, and this attention is available when used in prayer. She suggests that students should not be too choosy about the subjects they study or anxious about how well they do in a certain subject. Instead, they should be more focused on developing their faculty of attention which when "directed toward God is the very substance of prayer." Since prayer is the soul's orientation to God, then the quality of prayer is subjected to the attention given to God.[18]

The twin gifts of indifference and attentiveness will pave the way for us to be free. They will lead us to the realization of the true, authentic self. We are free when we are indifferent to the compulsions of life which the false self craves. When detached from such inclinations, we begin to be attentive to the few things that count for life; those things that make us more human. We begin to value relationships, justice, truth and service of others. To Jean Vanier, the road to freedom involves the gifts of indifference and attentiveness:

> We set out on the road to freedom when we no longer let our compulsions or passions govern us. We are freed when we begin to put justice, heartfelt relationships, and service of others and of truth over and above our own needs for love and success or our fears for failure and of relationships.[19]

There is a story of a monk who found a precious stone during his travels. He kept the stone inside his bag. One day, he met a fellow traveler who noticed the precious stone in his bag when he opened it to share some of his provisions with him. He then asked the monk to give it to him. To his surprise, the monk did so without much hesitation. The traveler, overjoyed with his new found wealth, quickly departed for home. The precious stone was enough to give him riches and security for a long time. However, a few days later, he came back to search for the monk. He found

---

18. Weil, *Waiting For God*, 57–65.
19. Vanier, *Becoming Human*, 115.

the monk and gave the precious stone back to him. Upon returning the stone, he made one more request from the monk, "Now give me something much more precious than this stone, valuable as it is. Give me that which enabled you to give it to me."[20]

The traveler in the story is wise enough to see that freedom is more precious than all the wealth in the world. If a man is not free, he denies his humanity. To be free is to be truly human.

Questions to Consider and Reflect

1. Why is it difficult, for many of us, to spend a short time in solitude and silence? Think of some ways you can experience solitude and silence in your busy life.
2. Have you ever experienced the power of silence in your life? Can you think of an experience you have with silence that made an impact to your life?
3. Have you ever experienced the "dark night" in your Christian life? How was the experience like, and how did you get out of it?

---

20. McGrath, *The Unknown God*, 47.

Chapter 4

Being Truly Human

> If you want a good litmus test of your spiritual growth, simply examine the nature and quality of your relationships with others.
>
> —Robert Mulholland Jr.[1]

Freedom to Love

A STUDENT ONCE TOLD me that I was more human. I wasn't sure what she meant by that. Maybe I was more accommodating than the other teachers because I was giving her a day off from class due to a domestic situation. What she said struck a chord in me, and I took this as a compliment. Indeed God had been transforming my life since I began practicing the desert way of spiritual formation. The desert way enables a person to be free from the compulsions of the false self in order for the true self to emerge. No longer nagged by the compulsive self to control, to seek approval, to compare and compete; he is free to be truly human.

What does it mean to be truly human? It means to be free from the need to cater to the false, egoistic self. When we are not longer governed by the compulsions, we are free to deal with

---

1. Mulholland Jr., *Invitation to a Journey*, 42.

ourselves in a truthful manner. We do not need to hide under a homemade identity, shy away from our own brokenness, or fearful of our weaknesses. The capacity to love ourselves and others is greater because we are no longer preoccupied with mending or upgrading our self-image. Freedom is a condition for authentic love. If we love without freedom, we love out of the ego. We are not free to love if we are still anxious of our self-worth that needs propping up from time to time. Alan Jones is right when he says that sometimes we love out of the inner cravings for control, security, and affection. These cravings masquerade as love, but they are counterfeits.[2]

We used to have two dogs at home. Their names were Shepherd and Milo. Both were small pinschers. Shepherd was a runt dog: slightly deformed and walked with a limp. We took her out of pity because nobody would want her. Milo was a handsome, obedient, and intelligent pinscher. Both dogs loved to run up and play on the grassy slope behind our house. When we called their names, Milo would be the first to run down the slope, but Shepherd stubbornly ignored us and did her own thing. Milo would go up and nudge her to come down while we waited below. It was natural for us to favor Milo over the other dog. We loved Milo more because she gave us delight and pleasure. We loved Shepherd less for obvious reasons—she gave us pain and anxiety. Our love was not authentic because it was conditioned by our need for control and affection. In this case, love becomes manipulative because we lack the freedom to love. Often we love in order to maintain a good conscience, to feel good, to get something out of another person, to show how good we are, or to receive praise and commendation from others.

---

2. Jones, *Soul Making*, 132.

Giving Attention to Another

What then is genuine love? Genuine love seeks to connect with others by giving attention to their worth as persons. Love is to give attention to the neighbor as highlighted in the story of the Good Samaritan. The priest and the Levite avoid the wounded person by the roadside because they are paying more attention to their own needs. If they stop to help, they may risk being a victim too; they may lose precious time; their program disrupted; or they will be financially liable. Because of their attentiveness to their own needs, they are not able to help those in need. Simone Weil who worked with the oppressed workers, poor miners, and vine workers, made this observation:

> Those who are unhappy have no need for anything in this world but people capable of giving them their attention. The capacity to give one's attention to a sufferer is a very rare and difficult thing; it is almost a miracle; it is a miracle.[3]

As a teacher, I remind myself that my teaching style must reflect genuine love which calls for mutual trust and respect. Teaching is more than a communication of knowledge; it is a communion of truth. Truth is best taught and transmitted relationally. We need a learning space for truth to be taught and obeyed. A relational space of trust and mutual respect is where students are not afraid to reveal their ignorance and the teacher secured enough to take questions. In such a non-threatening and non-judgmental environment, true learning takes place because the goal is obedience to the truth and not only to get and master information. According to Parker Palmer, truth is best discerned corporately among students and teacher (each person learning from the other) than through authoritative pronouncements by the teacher alone.[4] A teacher comes to class thinking that he is the expert on the subject. All the students need to do is to take

---

3. Weil, *Waiting for God*, 114.
4. Palmer, *To Know as We are Known*, 78.

in everything he has to say and cough them out at the end in the form of a test or assignment. Teachers who leave little space for the students to grow in their learning disturb me. They subject the students to their rigid style of teaching with little room to maneuver. This teaching may result in good grades but will not transform lives. Recently a graduating student came to me and shook my hand. Speaking in Chinese, she said, "Teacher, thank you for your life." We need to teach not only with words but with our life as well. Truth, no matter how painful and uninviting, is best conveyed and modeled relationally.

Manifestations of Humility

In order to show genuine love, we need humility. Humility is a way of life to the desert Christian. In the famous Rule of Benedict that dictates the way of living for the monks, the chapter on humility is placed right in the middle of the Rule. As Joan Chittister, herself a Benedictine nun, points out that the chapter "leavens the entire document, the entire way of life." [5] The humility of the desert is manifested in a willingness to learn from others and an unwillingness to stand in judgment of others.[6]

Desert Christians seriously take the challenge of Jesus to learn from him for he is gentle and humble of heart. How can God teach them? They see Jesus in their neighbor whom God can use to teach them "to act justly and to love mercy and to walk humbly with your God."[7] Abba Arsenius was a man of learning who received the best classical education available. He was once a personal tutor to the emperor's children. One day, the monks were shocked when they saw him seeking advice from an Egyptian peasant about his thoughts. "How is it that you, with such good Latin and Greek education, ask this poor peasant about

---

5. Chittister, *Wisdom Distilled from the Daily*, 52.
6. Williams, "Gentle and Humble of Heart," 10–13.
7. Mic 6:8.

your thoughts?" they asked him. He replied saying, "I have indeed been taught Latin and Greek, but I do not know even the alphabet of this peasant."[8]

It takes humility to learn from others. Humility opens a space for the other party to speak and calls us to enter into obedience to him or her. This requires us to listen well and pay attention to the speaker. The humble person is present to the other party without setting an agenda or giving judgment. She is not swift to cut in with her own views or offer help with the perceived problems. We can still learn without humility. Such learning makes one proud. Knowledge bloats the mind but famishes our soul. This kind of learning will not teach us how to act justly, love mercy, and walk humbly before God.

One way to know whether we have humility is the way we connect with people. One day I talked to a friend who was an intelligent and well-informed person. He heard about my wife's illness and came to encourage me. Despite his good intentions, I found it hard to be consoled by him. He was not there to listen. Rather his words pushed me to a corner with no room to breathe. He did not give me the space I needed because he made me feel that he knew better than me. The entire conversation was not helpful and a waste of time. Charles Ringma, professor of missions and evangelism at Regent College, has this advice for those who wants to draw close to enter into the place of pain.

> Going there does not mean barging in with easy answers and quick solutions. It means learning to listen even for what, initially, cannot be expressed…It means being there, but not controlling or crowding others. It means reaching out without taking over. It means holding without withholding, giving without looking to receive, and entering a partnership that releases others to pursue their own dreams and aspirations.[9]

---

8. Ward, *The Sayings of the Desert Fathers*, 10.
9. Ringma, *Dare to Journey with Henri Nouwen*, Reflection 11.

The other manifestation of humility is the unwillingness to judge others. This is to obey the words of Jesus who calls on us not to judge or we will be judged.[10] One day, Abba Moses was called by the elders to an assembly in order to punish a brother who was guilty of a certain sin. He refused to enter the assembly. A priest went to him urging him to come for the whole assembly was waiting for his presence. Then he arose taking with him an old, leaky basket filled with sand. He entered the assembly with the basket behind him. The assembly of brothers went out to meet him and saw the basket. "What is this, Father?" they asked. The old man replied, "My sins are running behind me and I do not see them, and I have come today to judge the sins of another man." When they heard these words, they were touched and forgave the sinning brother.[11]

Humility is Truthful Living

Humility calls us to face the truth and act on what we know is true. Truthful living is risky, and truthful telling is tough in a society that thrives on vanity and pride. We know the classic story of the emperor with no clothes. In this story, the emperor is a proud and vain man whose passion in life is to wear the finest clothes he can find. He spares no expenses to find them. Three conmen, on hearing about the emperor's passion, decide to play a trick on him in order to teach him a good lesson. They disguise themselves as tailors from afar and claim to sew the most beautiful garments that only the wise can see. The unwise and dumb will not be able to see and appreciate them. The emperor gives the go-ahead. The tailors pretend to sew for several days. Finally the garment is ready. The emperor, proudly wearing his "invisible" clothes, goes on parade. This is for the citizens to view and admire this exquisite display. The citizens, not wanting to

---

10. Matt 7:1.
11. Waddell, *The Desert Fathers*, 101–2.

appear foolish, comment positively on the emperor's clothes. The emperor, not wanting to act dumb, plays along with the cheering crowd. Everything goes along well until a child's voice is heard above the noise of the crowd. The innocent child, pointing his finger at the emperor, speaks loudly to his mother saying, "The emperor has no clothes on!"

Adults find it difficult to speak the truth for fear of the consequences. The citizens are not willing to tell the truth for fear of appearing dumb before others due to pride in their hearts. They also do not want to hurt the feelings of the emperor, for they know that he is an extremely proud person. Because of pride, which is the antithesis of humility, truthful living is not easy. Are we willing to let people point out our faults? Are we ready to face our own nakedness and appear weak and vulnerable? Do we sincerely want to face the truth and act on what is true? This takes courage on our part. It takes humility.

According to Bernard of Clairvaux, abbot and founder of the Cistercian order in the twelfth century, humility requires us to take constant steps to grow in truth.[12] The first step is to know the truth about ourselves. We have to face the truth that we are creatures with a sinful nature in need of the redeeming love of God. We will not grow in humility until we face our brokenness and embrace the pain that comes with it. We tend to be defensive over our mistakes, to make excuses to cover up our faults, or to pass the blame to others for our shortcomings. How often do we find people who are willing to own up to their mistakes and take steps to remedy them? Pride will not allow this to happen.

The next step is to know the truth about our neighbors. Knowing who we are—weak, vulnerable, and impoverished creatures—will help us to know our neighbors as we both share a common humanity. This enables us to show compassion to them. According to Catherine of Siena, charity or compassionate love is nursed and mothered by humility. We have compassion when we feel the pain of the other person as our own. Those who are

---

12. Cited by Pennington, "Bernard's Challenge" 21–23.

willing to face the wounds in their hearts will be able to identify and feel the same wounds in another person. The writer to Hebrews reminds us that Christ sympathizes with our weaknesses because he too faced his own weaknesses in every way. It is by the wounds of Christ that we receive healing as proclaimed by the prophet Isaiah.

The last step is to know the truth about God. Jesus says that only the pure in heart can know God. The heart becomes pure and free of self-deception when it is willing to confront the truth about self and others in contemplative prayer to God. A heart free of the illusions of self allows itself to dwell with God in the full embrace of his love. Such a life lived in humility will impact others. Others will experience themselves as the beloved of God in the presence of such people. Having met Mother Theresa, Basil Pennington can testify to this:

> This morning I sat across the table and looked into the eyes of Mother Theresa in Calcutta that is forever etched in my soul. That morning I came to know, love, and respect myself as a Christ-person, the beloved of God.[13]

Hospitality is to Make Ourselves Available

Besides humility, genuine love also needs charity or hospitality. Gerald Sittser in his book, *Water from a Deep Well*, points out that the goal of inner transformation for the desert saints is the manifestation of humility and charity which are considered to be the highest of virtues.[14] A young disciple came asking his master, "How do I find God?" He continued, "Do I need to fast, to labor, and to keep vigils?" The master responded that many practiced the disciplines but to no profit because they lacked discretion. "Even if our mouths stink from fasting, and we have learned all

---

13. Pennington, "Bernard's Challenge" 23.
14. Sittser, *Water from a Deep Well*, 91.

the Scriptures, and memorize the whole Psalter, we still lack what God wants—humility and charity."[15]

Hospitality is the most concrete form of charity. It is a virtue that belongs prominently to the desert. The need for mutual dependence in a wild, isolated place filled with unseen dangers and hardship fosters hospitality. It is a matter of mutual survival. No stranger is turned away in such an unforgiving environment with the mutual understanding that the same treatment will be given in return when needed in the future. Bedouin hospitality is legendary. If the guest comes on horseback, the Bedouin will first ask to feed his horse himself. The guest will then be invited to the tent for coffee. The master of the tent will personally prepare the coffee by roasting the beans over the fire and letting it cool in a wooden dish. When pounded into powder, the beans are boiled with cardamom. Three cups of coffee are prepared for this occasion. The master tastes the first cup (*el-heif*) to make the guest feel safe. The guest tastes the second cup (*el-keif*). The guest then drinks the third cup (*el-dheif*) and empties it before giving it back to the host. He is under the protection of the host the moment he consumes the coffee.

Lot, who previously lived in tents before Sodom, understood this very well. He would do anything to protect his two guests (actually angels) from those outside his door in Sodom. The men of Sodom, who were homosexuals, wanted sex with the two strangers that Lot had taken into his home. The crowd outside became rowdy and called for Lot to bring them out. Lot went outside to meet the unruly crowd calling on them not to do any harm to his guests, "for they have come under the protection of my roof."[16]

Hospitality is more than sharing a meal or providing a bed for a guest. It is more an attitude, a habit of the heart, than action. "It is," as Christine Pohl says in her book, *Making*

---

15. Cited by Sittser, *Water*, 91.
16. Gen 19:8.

Room, "a welcome with dispositions characterized by love and generosity."[17] It is more about making a room in our heart than finding a room in our house. It is to make ourselves available by giving the other person our undivided attention without imposing on him. John Cassian and Germanus once travelled to Egypt to visit a monk. They also noticed that the monk broke his rule of fasting while they were welcomed and shown hospitality. Out of curiosity they asked him, "Why when you welcome us, you do not keep to the rule of fasting as they do in Palestine?" The monk replied, "Fasting is always at hand but you I cannot have with me always. Furthermore, fasting is certainly a useful and necessary thing, but it depends on our choice while the law of God lays it upon us to do the works of charity. Thus, receiving Christ in you, I ought to serve you with diligence, but when I have taken leave of you, I can resume the rule of fasting again."[18]

Hospitality is to make ourselves available and be fully present to the other person. This is not easy, for we often receive people with a divided mind. Sue Monk Kidd points this out:

> To be fully present is not to pass judgment on the other person, wanting to convert her to our point of view, desiring her appreciation, wondering what others may think, worrying about the weather, or generally getting caught up in one's own feelings, desires, and opinions of the moment.[19]

It is difficult to create a space for people when our life is tied to a busy schedule, or when our minds are filled with the daily affairs of life that need our immediate attention. Jean Vanier confesses that, at times, even when he invites people into his office to talk, he makes clear to them in small ways that he is busy and has to attend to other things. He writes, "The door of my office is

---

17. Pohl, *Making Room*, 152.
18. Ward, *The Sayings of the Desert Fathers*, 113.
19. Kidd, "Live Welcoming to All," 9.

open, but the door of my heart is closed."[20] We tend to use busyness as an excuse for the lack of availability to attend to others.

Who can be busier than Jesus? One time Jesus went to Jairius's house to attend to his dying daughter. The request of the father was urgent. The crowd sensed the urgency and followed closely by pressing behind Jesus. The woman knew that Jesus had no time for her. She only wanted to touch him and did not expect an audience from the busy rabbi. Jesus stopped in his track and made himself available to the suffering woman. Which was more urgent to Jesus? Surely attending to a dying person was more urgent. Jesus would have ruined his reputation by delaying because Jairus was a ruler of the synagogue much respected by the local people. The urgent matter had to wait. Jesus created a space for the woman to tell her story. He looked at the woman; his eyes told her that he was there to listen to her story and share her pain without judgment and criticism. In the hospitable space given by Jesus, she found the freedom and courage to tell the painful truth and to confront her suffering that was in her heart for a long time. She heard these consoling words from Jesus saying, "Daughter, your faith has healed you. Go in peace and be freed from your suffering."[21] A change had taken place in the hospitable space created by Jesus. She had shalom. Healing had gone beyond her physical condition to her whole person. She was now able not only to enjoy good physical health but also a healthy relationship with herself, others, and God.

The virtues of hospitality and humility cannot be separated. They are twins. We cannot have one without the other. To make ourselves attentive and be available to others is to submit to them. It means to let the other party dictate to us how we should use our time and resources. I often meet people who are willing to offer help provided it does not cause them any inconvenience. I remember, at one time, we were looking for a place to stay in Singapore. A couple, who happened to be on a mission trip to

20. Vanier, *Community and Growth*, 267.
21. Mark 5:34.

Cambodia, offered their place to us during their time out of the country. We were glad for this opportunity and took up the offer. We went into a depressed mood when we arrived at the place. At every turn (in the bedroom, kitchen, bathroom), a long list of "dos and don'ts" rules (pasted on the wall or door) greeted us. We could only use the fan and not the air-conditioner. We need to switch off the lights and fan whenever we leave the room or house. We have to keep the place clean. We must save and minimize the use of water. The following day we decided to leave for another place to stay.

Hospitality in Different Worlds[22]

We belong to different worlds and move in and out of different relationships all the time. Part of our being human, as Jean Vanier points out, is that we cannot live in a solitary state. We need to connect, out of mutual dependency, with others and learn to belong.[23] The home, school, and workplace are the different worlds that we belong on a daily basis. These are where we can carve out a hospitable space for our children, guests, students, and colleagues.

First, we need to look at hospitality at the home. Hospitality is a trademark of the Christian's identity. Inviting people to stay in the home has biblical precedence. The Lord appeared to Abraham at the great trees of Mamre. Abraham saw three men standing nearby while he was sitting at the entrance of his tent. The day was hot, so Abraham invited the three men to his home and said to them: "Let a little water be brought, and then you may all wash your feet and rest under this tree. Let me get you something to eat, so that you can be refreshed and then go on your way."[24]

---

22. I am indebted to Henri Nouwen for the concept of hospitality in different places. See his book, *Reaching Out*, 79–90.

23. Vanier, *Becoming Human*, 41.

24. Gen 18:4–5.

This story of hospitality is depicted in a famous masterpiece called "Holy Trinity" by a monk named Andrei Rublev in 1411 A.D. during a period of trouble and discord in Russian history. The subject of Rublev's icon focuses on three angels, disguised as travelers, enjoying Abraham's hospitality under the shade of the trees of Mamre. In this painting, the artist is portraying a vision of harmony and peace as depicted by the three Persons of the Godhead in one accord—the Trinity. Like all icons, the main object is to draw the viewer into the story of the painting and be part of the scene. The three angelic figures incline towards each other in endless, silent conversation. A circular, hospitable space is created between them. The centerpiece of the hospitable space is the Eucharist cup; it invites the viewer to share in the hosts' welcome and generous love poured out for many through the sacrifice of Christ. The icon induces us to worship God with a grateful heart. Christine Pohl is right when she says that hospitality is a response of a thankful heart in the light of God's love and welcome to us.[25] It is out of this gratefulness that led Chrysostom, archbishop in Constantinople in the fourth century, to instruct his people to "make for yourself a guest chamber in your own house: set up a bed there, set up a table there, and a candlestick... Have a room to which Christ may come; say, "This is Christ's cell; this building is set apart for him."[26]

Children, who should be treated as guests in the home, need a safe and secure place to grow up. The home should be a hospitable place, but unfortunately this is not the case in many homes. Many children come from broken homes where conflict and strife have squeezed out the space needed for wholesome and healthy growth. They lack a hospitable environment that allows them to be equipped with the character, wisdom, strength, and freedom to stand on their own feet before an inhospitable world out there. The biblical concept of a blessed home is where

---

25. Pohl, *Making Room*, 172.

26. Cited by Pohl, *Making Room*, 154. See Chrysostom, "Homily 45 on Acts" 277.

children are trained as "polished arrows" to shoot straight and to contend with the enemies at the gate.[27] For this to happen, a home needs a hospitable space. It is a safe place where children can grow and develop without the fear of criticism and rejection. It is a non-threatening place where children feel secure to ask the wrong questions and to make mistakes without fear of judgment or punishment. The home is not a place without boundaries. A safe and secure place needs fencing. The child needs to be protected from harm while enjoying the space. A child must be taught what he can and cannot do. Setting limits will help the child curb with his appetites and desires. This will train his character development and teach him to respect the space of others.

Next, we need to look at hospitality at school. Some years ago my wife was tutoring a child who hated school. He loved animals, and his favorite animal was the lion. He had a toy lion at home named Alex; he talked to his toy like a close friend. One day my wife asked him to draw a picture that he liked. He drew a lion eating up a man. The drawing shocked my wife, and she asked who the man in the picture was. He told her that the man was a teacher in his school. Many of us can recall some painful experiences with teachers at school. When we were young and naive, we were fearful of our teachers. They looked like giants, and we tended to call them by all sorts of names based on our perceptions of them. When I was in primary school, I had a physical education teacher who liked to instill fear on his students. On the first day of class, he took a huge ruler and wacked it hard on a desk in front of him in order to frighten the students. He told us that he would not hesitate to use his "weapon" on anyone who disobeyed his marching orders. We dislike school because they can make life difficult for us. Once a while, we meet a teacher we like because her presence does not intimidate us. She has given us a space in our hearts to grow and develop. She is someone that we remember for as long as we live.

---

27. Psalm 127: 4-5.

Being Truly Human

Parker Palmer warns that words used by teachers can close up the learning space because students do not want to reveal their ignorance and be embarrassed before their peers.[28] For students to learn well, without fear or intimidation, a hospitable space is needed. Unfortunately this is not happening in schools in East Asia. The concept that the teacher knows best is prevalent in many cultures. Teachers are quick to offer answers to problems raised in order to prove their authority and expertise. Sometimes, in order to maintain their invincibility in class, teachers do not encourage meaningful discourse. The learning process is always one sided. Boundaries are set to make sure this happens; they will be penalized if they step over the line. The "good" students are those who toe the line in order to please the teacher. The more adventurous students who prefer to throw in their own ideas are penalized. This style of teaching will not open up a learning space for students to learn and obey truth.

Lastly, we look at hospitality at the workplace. Henry Ford, the renowned American pioneer in mass production using the assembly line strategy, used to make this complaint: how is it that he always has to engage a man or a woman when all he needs is a pair of hands? He will have his wish fulfilled if he is alive today. The robotic arm in car factories takes over the pair of human hands. The question is revealing because companies, by and large, show interest not in the worker as a person but in the bottom line: productivity and profitability. The worker can be easily replaced like cogs in a machine if he is not productive. Fortunately humans who can get sick and have moods are not machines. Unlike machines, they can also lead, innovate, create, love, serve, and hate. William Pollard, the chairman of Service-Master, makes this observation:

> But people have the potential to improve upon their knowledge, to modify, to adapt, and to exercise judgment within a framework of moral values. It is not just what we

---

28. Palmer, *To Know As We Are Known*, 74.

are doing, but what we are becoming in the process that gives us distinct value and is uniquely human.[29]

Pollard's firm is committed not only to excellence and profitability but also to people development. A hospitable space is created for the worker to grow and develop his potential. It is a space where commitment goes both ways. The worker is committed to giving quality work for his company, and the firm is committed to the welfare and growth of its workers. Both, through their commitments, are adding value to each other. Pollard's firm finds out that the employee tends to be more loyal and committed to the company when there is an environment that favors the worker.

Max DePree, chairman of a furniture company, sees the need to recognize and tap the full potential of his workers. In his acclaimed book, *Leadership is an Art*, he notes that a leader should be able to liberate people to do what is required of them in the most effective and humane way. For example, in his firm each worker who has an idea to contribute should be taken seriously. Leaders who endorse the concept that people are different and diverse in gifts, talent, and skills are trained to listen carefully to the followers and respond to them creatively. Each worker is unique and plays a necessary, important role in the company. Leaders should have the confidence to "encourage contrary opinions," and "to abandon themselves to the strength of others."[30]

Most of us view work in purely remunerative terms. The parable of the vineyard workers will give us a different perspective on work. In the parable, the early batch of workers receives the same salary as the last batch that works only for one hour. The early batch of workers is not happy and complains, for they work for money. They think they deserve to be paid more for the hours they work in comparison to the last batch. The last batch is happy that they can find work the last minute. They stand the whole

---

29. Pollard, *The Soul of the Firm*, 26.
30. DePree, *Leadership is an Art*, xx.

day, under the hot sun, waiting to be employed. For them, work gives dignity. The owner of the vineyard pays all the workers the same salary to bring home the point: work that gives a person the means to use his gifts and tap his potential is what makes him human. Hospitality, in the workplace, requires us to treat people with respect and dignity.

Hospitality to the Marginalized

My wife works at a center for homeschoolers. The children will come to the center to be supervised in their school work. The supervisors are there to make sure they do the assigned work for the day and to help them in their school work. This center is different from the usual school because it allows each student to learn at her own pace. It is not unusual to have a mixed group of students, with different age groups and learning levels, to stay in the same class. Some students who are marginalized by the mainstream because of learning disabilities find a home at the center. The church-run center maintains a policy of inclusion by taking in autistic and slow learners. The mainstream schools, public or private, do not cater to people who live at the fringe.

    The marginalized and downtrodden are considered misfits in mainstream society. Why does society at large exclude these people? Jean Vanier, who found L'Arche, an international network of communities for people with intellectual disabilities, contends that the root cause of this prejudice is fear.[31] There are several reasons for this fear. If society includes them, the people fear that this will upset their lifestyle, cost them time and money, affect their social status, and draw criticism from friends and relatives. Hence to include the marginalized is risky business, and few people will want to take this risk.

    If fear excludes these people, then trust is needed to open a space in the hearts for the marginalized. Trust is not easily

---

31. Vanier, *Becoming Human*, 73.

available because, from a young age, we learn mostly through fear. The fear of rejection keeps us wanting to please others. The fear of failure makes us competitive and wanting to succeed. The fear of ridicule forbids us from taking risks. The fear of shame prevents us from opening up our lives to other people. We begin to see them differently when we learn to overcome these fears and open a hospitable space in our hearts for such people. We realize that they are people like us with genuine needs. Their fears reveal our fears; their weaknesses reflect our vulnerability; their frustration speaks to our frustration.

When I read the Scripture, I begin to see that God gauges our spirituality not primarily on how much we spend time in prayer, or how well we do the disciplines, or how many ministries we serve in the church, or how many souls we won to Christ, but on how much we include the marginalized and downtrodden in our life. Many times Jesus ministered to people on the fringe: the woman with a blood disease; social outcasts like the leper, the lame, the blind, and the dumb; the Samaritan woman; the demon-possessed; tax-collectors; woman caught in adultery; and many more. The prophet Isaiah, knowing that the worshippers' hearts were not open to those in distress, cried out when he saw them going to the temple to fast and offered sacrifices:

> Is not this the kind of fasting I have chosen: to loose the chains of injustice and untie the cords of the yoke, to set the oppressed free and break every yoke? Is it not to share your food with the hungry and to provide the poor wanderer with shelter—when you see the naked, to clothe him . . . ?[32]

We enter the desert to rediscover who we are. We do not enter the desert to escape from the world and its problems. We are ready to find a way back to serve the community when we are in touch with our true identity. Meister Eckhart writes that true contemplation in the desert will reap a harvest of action in

32. Isa 58: 6–7.

the world.[33] When we are detached and not polluted by worldly compulsions, we are free to play a constructive and effective role in making the world a better place, with little expectations of results or rewards in return.

Thomas Merton understands what it means to be truly human. His advice to a young social activist clearly reflects this understanding. He knows the dangers of engagement with the world. He cautions him to be careful with the way he views his activities in the world. He can be so caught up with his own ideals about doing the right thing and going for results that he misses what is essentially important in his kind of work. His concern with how he is doing reveals his fears of failure and a sense of nothingness. He may be tempted to use his engagement with the world to build his own self-identity. According to Merton, this is not the right way to view his work. If he views his involvement in this way, he can get easily disappointed. At the end of the day, what is essential is his love for truth and people. If he genuinely has love then all work becomes meaningful and true. In a letter to James Forest in 1966, he writes:

> Do not depend on the hope of results. When you are doing the sort of work you have taken on, essentially an apostolic work, you may have to face the fact that your work will be apparently worthless and achieve no result at all, if not perhaps results opposite to what you expect. As you get used to this idea, you start more and more to concentrate not on the results but on the value, the truth of the work itself. And there, too, a great deal has to be gone through, as gradually as you struggle less and less for an idea and more and more for specific people. The range tends to narrow down, but it gets much more real. In the end, it is the reality of personal relationships that save everything . . . The big results are not in your hands or mine, but they suddenly happen, and we can share in them, but there is no point in building our lives on this personal satisfaction, which may be denied us and

---

33. Meister Eckhart, "German Sermon 3" 111.

which after all is not that important...You are probably striving to build yourself an identity in your work, out of your work and witness. You are using it, so to speak, to protect yourself against nothingness, annihilation. That is not the right use of your work. All the good that you will do will come, not from you but from the fact that you have allowed yourself, in the obedience of faith, to be used by God's love. Think of this more and gradually you will be free from the need to prove yourself, and you can be more open to the power that will work through you without your knowing it . . . [34]

Conclusion

Mr. Bean, the British comedian, is planning to go on a trip. He has all the things ready for the trip: clothes, shoes, suntan lotion, soap, toothpaste, and towels. He soon finds out that his bag is too small for all the stuff that he wants to bring along. He has a fantastic idea. He cuts his long pants into shorts; he presses out half of the tube of toothpaste; he breaks his toothbrush into two; he does the same thing to the rest of his stuff reducing them into half the size or volume. He is now able to put all things into the luggage bag. As he puts his bag away, he notices that he has another identical bag tucked away in a corner of the room which is twice the size of the first bag. While biting his lips and scratching his head, Mr. Bean is thinking hard about his newly discovered dilemma. Suddenly he has an idea. With glee, he puts the smaller bag into the bigger bag and off he goes. We laugh at the silly way of doing things, but the lesson is clear. It makes sense for us to travel with as little baggage as possible. As we travel through life, our baggage becomes bigger and heavier. We tend to pick things along the way, and our life is getting more complicated—filled with activities, things, ideas, worries, and addictions. Belden Lane, a keen backpacker himself, has this to say:

---

34. Merton, *The Hidden Ground of Love*, 294.

> Backpackers learn, sometimes the hard way that simplicity is always a question of knowing what to leave behind. This is a desert truth, translatable to the rest of one's life as well . . . How much can you leave behind? This is the desert's question.[35]

The desert way of spiritual formation challenges us to travel with less. The stinginess of the desert, besides space, is its characteristic mark. Reflecting the outward desert, we too need to be relieved of the excess baggage in our life. The author of the book of Hebrews reminds us to throw away anything that hinders us from running the race for God.[36] The complexity of life in the modern consumer world that thrives on more and more is incompatible with our spiritual endeavors. There is little space for God in our heart when life is filled to the brim.

Our life is packed with activities. In order to make full use of our time, we run from one activity to another. Since we thrive on doing rather than being, this running about gives us a good feeling. We feel guilty, bored, and useless if we are not maximizing our time. The efficient use of time leads us to appreciate multitasking. We envy those who can juggle and do several things at one time. I am amazed at those people who are busy taking calls while driving. Too much activity can suffocate the spiritual life. The Bible says that we need to be still in order to know God. The churches and Christians may not realize that much activity can do more harm than good to their spiritualities. G. K. Chesterton, writer and Christian apologist, is disturbed when he sees people destroying their hard-won holidays by doing something and filling in the time with some relevant activity. In his *Autobiography*, he writes, "For my part, I never can get enough Nothing to do."[37]

Our life is cluttered with things. We usually have more things than we need. Under the lure of clever advertising and pressure from the Joneses, we acquire things even though we do

35. Lane, *The Solace of Fierce Landscapes*, 166.
36. Heb 12:1
37. Cited by Lane, *The Solace of Fierce Landscapes*, 82.

not need them or cannot afford them. We fall prey to easy credit and the power of consumerism unless we consciously resist the temptation to hoard. The Bible warns us about serving two masters. We either serve God or Mammon. There is only enough space in our hearts for one of them. Our love for material things will lead us astray from the path we are taking. The reason is that we need money to maintain a materialistic lifestyle. We spend most of our energy and time chasing after the Almighty Dollar than the God we trust.

Our life is filled with worries. The stress of modern living is making us nervous and anxious. Modernity is more prevalent and concentrated in cities than in rural areas. I am amazed by the carefree life of the villagers. Once I was at Stone Drum Village in Yunnan, China. It is an ancient place situated at the first bend of the Yangtze River. This place is made famous in history because Maoist soldiers, during the Long March, crossed the river in order to evade the Nationalists. This event is inscribed on a stone shaped like a drum that gives the village its name. There is even a small museum to commemorate the event. When I was there, an old lady who happened to see us as we walked up the village invited us to have tea with her. Later, she even persuaded us to have lunch with her family when her daughter-in-law came back from a nearby school for her lunch break. She gave us some of her homemade pickled chilies as a parting gift when we left her home. She treated us like old friends even though we were strangers to her. On the other hand, we treat strangers with suspicion in the city. We constantly worry over our safety and take security measures to prevent strangers entering our homes.

Our life is full of words and ideas. Living in a wordy world, we freely dispense our opinions without reservation. Sometimes we regret having been so casual with our thoughts or remarks. New technology makes this possible. Social media platforms, like *Facebook* and *Twitter*, provide the avenues for people, across the globe, to interact with each other by making private comments in the public arena. We like to make our opinions known to the world at the first opportunity. A Zen story goes like this. Once, a university professor visited a Zen master to ask about Zen. The master served him tea by pouring it into his cup. He poured until the visitor's cup was overflowing with tea. The professor noticed the cup and said, "The cup is full and no more can go in!" The master looked at him and replied, "I know. Like this cup, you are full of opinions and speculations. How can I teach you Zen unless you first empty your cup?"[38]

And lastly, our life is drowned with addictions. When we think of addictions, we think of drugs or alcohol. Addictions can be as innocent as impulsive purchasing or a love for fast foods. Some addictions can affect or disrupt the ability to function normally. Other addictions will only affect the moods and sentiments. Life can be tough, and one way to avoid the anxiety and angst that come with living in an inhospitable world is to seek refuge in one's addictions. Such addictions will shield and numb us from the pain of the realities of life. Addictions will make us hang on to the illusions of life. We refuse to face our own pain and brokenness which life mercilessly offers us from time to time. We prefer to live in a world of dreams, illusions, and fantasies. Being truly human means that we need to live an authentic life grounded in reality.

A life full of activities, material things, worries, words and opinions, and addictions, is not conducive for the spiritual odyssey. Perhaps, this is the greatest hindrance and challenge for those of us who desire to embark on the journey in the wilderness of our souls. We need to take heed to the question posed by the desert to us, "How much can you leave behind?" We need to let go, and let the desert way of spirituality does its work of emptying our life.

---

38. Reps, *Zen Flesh, Zen Bones*, 5.

Questions to Consider and Reflect

1. Do you have the freedom to love? Is your love conditioned by the need for control and affection?

2. Hospitality is to make ourselves available and be fully present to the other person. How has this definition of hospitality change the way you deal with people?

3. What insights can you gain from Merton's advice to the young social activist? What is Merton's major concern when engaging ourselves with the world? How can you escape the trap of delusion in your work or activity?

4. What hindrances prevent you from embarking on this journey in the wilderness of your soul? Can you identify them? How do you propose to empty your life of these things that hinder your spiritual growth?

Appendix A

Silent Retreat: Making Space for God in Our Busy Lives

> The quieter the mind, the more powerful, the worthier, the deeper, the more telling and more perfect the prayer is.
>
> —MEISTER ECKHART[1]

THE PURPOSE OF THE silent retreat is to detach yourself from the world of noise and activities and get connected with God by giving him space in your mind and heart for him to speak to you. There are some steps you can take for this to happen:

1. Be attentive to your physical condition. Choose a nice, comfortable spot with the least distractions to have your personal retreat. Take deep breaths and listen to your body. Are you tired, anxious, restless or tense? Correct, deep breathing will help you to relax and calm your body.

2. Be attentive to the present moment. Use your senses to be fully present to what is happening at the present time. You can use your senses to smell the foliage around you; listen

---

1. Eckhart, *Whom God Hid Nothing*, 15.

to the sounds of nature; take in the sights of the scenery; feel your bodily movements; etc.

3. Be attentive to what God is saying to you.
   a. God speaks through nature. For example, think of a nearby rock, flower, or tree. How does the rock, flower, or tree speak to you about him?
   b. God speaks through scripture. You can use this time to study and meditate on selected passages of the bible. Another way is to let the bible speak to you using the *Lectio* method (see Appendix B).
   c. God speaks through events. With the help of the Holy Spirit and prayerful reflection, you can discern God's direction and guidance for yourself as you recall the events that happened to you recently.
   d. God speaks through the heart. One way to get in touch with your heart is to write down your thoughts and feelings in a journal, or express them in a poem, or use them to draw a picture.

It is not advisable to have a predetermined agenda for the retreat. Let God set the agenda. Come to the retreat with nothing more than a desire to meet God. Come with a prepared heart and not with a scheduled program. Leave your busy life behind and come to the retreat with nothing more than a bible, pen and paper. Simplicity is the key. Do not expect anything to happen during the retreat. Focus on God and not on the results. Usually the effects of it will come after the retreat is over, and you will find your spirit, mind, and soul realigned, refreshed, and renewed when you take time to be with God by giving him the space and time to enter your life once again.

Appendix B

The Practice of *Lectio Divina*

SILENT PRAYER CAN BE complemented with the practice of the prayerful reading of Scripture (*lectio divina*). This practice is different from our common understanding of bible reading. In bible reading, we study the text for the purpose of encouragement and edification. From the text, we may want to extract some principles that we can immediately apply to our life. In bible reading, the mind is active and fully engaged. In the prayerful reading of Scripture, we need to listen with our heart to the "still, small voice" of God that uses a word or phrase to speak to us. Through this, God is drawing us into his presence and guiding us to rest in him. To simply rest in God's embrace is the objective of praying the Scriptures. The practice involves four steps.

First, you need to choose a text of Scripture that you want to pray over. Make sure your body is relaxed and in a comfortable position. Some deep breathing may help you to relax and focus. Allow yourself to be silent for a time before the reading begins. Read the text slowly and reflectively. Do not hurry but let each word sinks in. After the first reading, allow a short period of silence. At the second reading, a word or phrase may impress or catch your attention. The word or phrase is God's gentle voice inviting you into his presence. At this stage, do not continue reading but move to the second stage.

Second, ponder over the word or phrase in your heart. Meditate, memorize, or repeat the word or phrase in your heart

Appendix B

until it speaks to your present situation. What area of your life has the word or phrase touches you? Now you know that God has used it to speak to your life what should be your response?

Third, you need to talk to God in prayer. This dialogue with God may not necessarily be verbal. What God has awakened in your heart, you need to offer it back to him. What is God calling you to do or become? What inner experience is God calling you? Say the prayer of praise and thanksgiving about these matters that arise in your heart.

Fourth, you need to enter into a state of silence and simply rest in his presence. Experience the quiet fullness of God's love and peace in your heart as you open yourself to him. Jesus promises you rest as you go to him.[2]

The prayerful or spiritual reading of Scripture is best summed up by Francois Fenelon:

> As to the subject of your meditations, take such passages of the Gospels or of *The Imitation of Christ*. Read slowly, and when a passage touches you, use it as you would a sweetmeat, which you hold in your mouth till it melts. Let the meaning sink slowly into your heart, and do not pass on to something else until you feel that to be exhausted . . . Trust God simply, like a child, in telling him whatever comes to your mind. The thing is to open your heart to God, to make it familiar with him, to strengthen it with love. Carefully fostered love, enlightens amends, corrects, encourages.[3]

---

2. Matt 11: 28–30.
3. Fenelon, "A Persevering Will to Pray," 38.

Bibliography for Further Reading

Abbey, Edward. *Desert Solitaire: A Season in the Wilderness.* New York: Ballantine, 1968.

Alighieri, Dante. *The Divine Comedy: Inferno.* Vol.1. Translated by Mark Musa. New York: Penguin, 1984.

Athanasius, "On the Incarnation," In *Library of Christian Classics,* Vol. III, Edited by Edward Roche Hardy. Philadelphia: Westminster, 1954.

Augustine, Saint, Bishop of Hippo. *The Confessions of Saint Augustine.* Translated with Introduction by E. M. Blaiklock. London: Hodder & Stoughton, 1983.

Barnes, M. Craig. *Searching for Home: Spirituality for Restless Souls.* Grand Rapids: Brazos, 2003.

Barton, Ruth Haley. *Invitation to Solitude and Silence: Experiencing God's Transforming Presence.* Downers Grove: IVP, 2004.

Benner, David G. *Soulful Spirituality: Becoming Fully Alive and Deeply Human,* Grand Rapids: Brazos, 2011.

Bloom, Anthony. *Beginning to Pray.* New York: Paulist, 1970.

Carretto, Carlo. *Letters from the Desert.* Translated by Rose Mary Hancock. Foreword by Ivan Illich. Maryknoll: Orbis, 1972.

Casey, Michael. *A Guide to Living in the Truth: Saint Benedict's Teaching on Humility.* Missouri: Liguori, 2001.

Chittister, Joan. *Wisdom Distilled from the Daily: Living the Rule of St. Benedict Today.* New York: HarperSanFrancisco, 1990.

Chrysostom, John. "Homily 45 on Acts," In *A Select Library of the Nicene and Post-Nicene Fathers of the Christian Church,* First Series (vol.11), Edited by Philip Schaff. New York: Christian Literature Company, 1886–90.

DePree, Max. *Leadership is an Art.* New York: Dell, 1989.

Dostoyevsky, Fyodor. *The Brothers Karamazo.* Translated by Andrew R. MacAndrew. New York: Bantam, 1970.

Eckhart, Meister. "German Sermon 39," In *Meister Eckhart: Teacher and Preacher.* Edited by Bernard McGinn. New York: Paulist, 1986.

———. *Whom God Hid Nothing.* Edited by David O'Neal. Boston: Shambhala, 1996.

———. "German Sermon 3," In *Meister Eckhart: A Modern Translation,* Edited by Raymond Blakney. New York: Harper & Brothers, 1941.

Fenelon, Francois, "A Persevering Will to Pray," *Weavings IV: 2* (1989) 38.

Bibliography for Further Reading

Foster, Richard. *Celebration of Discipline: The Path to Spiritual Growth.* London: Hodder & Stoughton, 1989.

Foucauld, Charles De. *Charles De Foucauld.* Writings Selected with an Introduction by Robert Ellsberg. New York: Orbis, 1999.

Giddens, Anthony. *Runaway World.* New York: Routledge, 2003.

Gorsuch, John P. *An Invitation to the Spiritual Journey.* New York: Paulist, 1990.

Hendricks, William D. *Exit Interviews: Revealing Stories of Why People are Leaving the Church.* Chicago: Moody, 1993.

Houston, James. *The Heart's Desire: A Guide to Personal Fulfillment.* Oxford: Lion, 1992.

John of the Cross. *The Collected Works of St. John of the Cross.* Translated by Kieran Kavanaugh and Otilio Rodriguez. New York: Doubleday, 1964.

Jones, Alan. *Soul Making: The Desert Way of Spirituality.* USA: HarperSanFrancisco, 1985.

Keating, Thomas. *The Human Condition: Contemplation and Transformation.* New York: Paulist, 1999.

———. *Open Mind, Open Heart: The Contemplation of the Gospel.* New York: Continuum, 2004.

Kelly, Thomas R. *A Testament of Devotion.* San Francisco: HarperSanFransico, 1996.

Kidd, Sue Monk. "Live Welcoming to All," *Weavings XII: 5* (1997) 9.

———. *God's Joyful Surprise.* San Francisco: Harper & Row, 1987.

Kierkegaard, Soren. *Christian Discourses.* London: Oxford University Press, 1940.

Lane, Belden C. *The Solace of Fierce Landscapes: Exploring Desert and Mountain Spirituality.* Oxford: Oxford University Press, 1998.

Lewis, C. S. *The Great Divorce.* New York: Macmillan, 1946.

McGrath, Alister. *The Unknown God.* Grand Rapids, MI: Eerdmans, 1999.

Mello, Anthony de. *One Minute Wisdom.* New York: Doubleday, 1988.

Merton, Thomas. "Wilderness and Paradise: Two Recent Studies," In *Cistercian Studies* 2:1 (1967).

———. *The Hidden Ground of Love,* Edited by William H. Shannon. New York: Farrar, Straus, Giroux, 1985.

Mulholland Jr., M. Robert. *Invitation to a Journey: A Road Map for Spiritual Formation.* Downers Grove: IVP, 1993.

Nouwen, Henri J.M. *Reaching Out: The Three Movements of the Spiritual Life.* New York: Image Books, 1975.

———. *The Way of the Heart: Desert Spirituality and Contemporary Ministry.* New York: Seabury, 1981.

———. *Life of the Beloved.* New York: Crossroad, 1992.

Pascal, Blaise. *Pensees.* Translated by John Warrington. London: J.M. Dent & Sons, 1973.

Palmer, Parker. *To Know as We are Known: Education as a Spiritual Journey.* New York: HarperSanFrancisco, 1993.

Pennington, Basil. "Bernard's Challenge," *Weavings XV: 3* (2000) 21–23.

Bibliography for Further Reading

Peterson, Eugene H. *Christ Plays in Ten Thousand Places*. Grand Rapids, MI: Eerdmans, 2005.

Pohl, Christine D., *Making Room: Recovering Hospitality as a Christian Tradition*. Grand Rapids, MI: Eerdmans, 1999.

Pollard . C. Willaims. *The Soul of the Firm*. Grand Rapids: Zondervan, 1996.

Reps, Paul. *Zen Flesh, Zen Bones*. Garden City: Doubleday, Anchor Books, 1961.

Ringma, Charles. *Dare to Journey with Henri Nouwen*. Colorado Springs: Pinon, 2000.

Shah, Idries et al. *Tales of the Dervishes*. New York: E. P. Dutton & Co., 1969.

Sittser, Gerald. *Water from a Deep Well*. Downers Grove, IL: IVP, 2007.

Stowell, Joseph M. *Moody Monthly,* (December,1989) 4.

Thoreau, Henry D. *Walden*. New York: Holt, Rinehart & Winston, 1963.

Vanier, Jean. *Becoming Human*. Toronto: Anansi, 1998.

———. *Community and Growth*. New York: Paulist, 1989.

Waddell, Helen. Translator. *The Desert Fathers*. New York: Vintage, 1998.

Walters, Kerry. *Soul Wilderness: A Desert Spirituality*. New York: Paulist, 2001.

Ward, Benedicta. *The Sayings of the Desert Fathers: The Alphabetical Collection*. Kalamazoo: Cistercian, 1975.

Warren, Robert. *The Practice of Prayer*. Grand Rapids: Baker, 2001.

Weil, Simone. *Waiting for God*. Translated by Emma Craufurd. New York: Perennial, 2001.

———. *The Need for Roots: Prelude to a Declaration of Duties Toward Mankind*. Translated by Arthur Willis. New York: Harper Colophon, 1971.

Williams, Michael E. "Gentle and Humble of Heart—Humility as a Response to Imperial Christianity." *Weavings XV: 3* (2000) 10-13.

Wolters, Clifton. Translator. *Cloud of Unknowing and Other Works*. England: Penguin, 1978.

www.ingramcontent.com/pod-product-compliance
Lightning Source LLC
Chambersburg PA
CBHW060421090426
42734CB00011B/2398